D1236093

The Rites of Christian Initiation

Historical and
Pastoral Reflections

Rev. Michel Dujarier

Translated and Edited
by Rev. Kevin Hart

Sadlier
A Division of William H. Sadlier, Inc.
New York
Chicago
Los Angeles

Nihil Obstat
Martin S. Rushford
Diocesan Censor
✠Imprimatur
Francis J. Mugavero, D.D.
Bishop of Brooklyn
Brooklyn, New York
October 15, 1979
The nihil obstat and imprimatur are official declarations that a book or pamphlet is free of doctrinal or moral error. No implication is contained therin that those who have granted the nihil obstat and imprimatur agree with the contents, opinions or statements expressed.

Ho

Y. 10007
9328-5
87654321

Contents

4

Patristic Sources

THE following works of the Fathers of the Church have been cited in this study. To avoid repetition in the footnotes, and to provide a convenient reference page for the reader, they are listed below. If no English translation for a particular work is listed, this is because the translator is not aware of any extant or easily available English translation. In this case the reader is referred to French translations, or the Latin original or translation. Note that the quotations from the Fathers in the text do not necessarily come from the translations listed below.

Ambrose

Theological and Dogmatic Works, translated by Roy J. Deferrari, Ph.D. Washington: The Catholic University of America Press, 1963. The Fathers of the Church. Contains *The Mysteries* and *The Sacraments.*

Augustine

Confessions, translated by Vernon J. Bourke. New York: Fathers of the Church, Inc., 1953, Vol. 5.

De fide et operibus, translated and annotated by the Rev. Gregory Joseph Lombardo, CSC. Washington: The Catholic University of America Press, 1950. Studies in Sacred Theology, second series, Vol. 47.

First Catechetical Instruction (De catechizandis rudibus), translated by Rev. Joseph P. Christopher. Westminster, Md.: Newman Press, 1946. Ancient Christian Writers.

On the Merits and Remission of Sins, and *On the Baptism of Infants (De peccatorum meritis et remissione,* and *De baptismo parvulorum),* edited by Philip Schaff. New York: The Christian Literature Company, 1887. The Nicene and Post-Nicene Fathers, Vol. 5: The Anti-Pelagian Writings, pp. 12-28.

The Sermons of Saint Augustine. Oxford: John H. Parker, 1844-45. A Library of the Fathers of the Holy Catholic Church. Vol. 1: Sermons 51-116; Vol. 2: Sermons 117-183.

Sermons on the Liturgical Seasons, translated by Sr. Mary Sarah Muldowney, RSM. New York: Fathers of the Church, Inc., 1959, Vol. 38. Contains homilies 184-265.

Clement of Alexandria

Alexandrian Christianity, selected translations, with introduction and notes by John Earnest Leonard Oulton and Henry Chadwick. Philadelphia: Westminster Press, 1954. Library of Christian Classics.

Christ the Educator (Paidagogus), translated by Simon P. Wood, C.P. New York: Fathers of the Church, Inc., 1954, Vol. 23.

The Miscellanies (Stromata), translated by Rev. William Wilson. Edinburgh: T. and T. Clark, 1869. Ante-Nicene Christian Library. Vol. 1: Books II-VIII; Vol. 2: Book I.

Cyprian, Bishop of Carthage

The Epistles of St. Cyprian, translated by H. Carey. Oxford: J. Parker. London: Rivingtons, 1844. A Library of the Fathers of the Holy Catholic Church.

Letters (1-81), translated by Sr. Rose Bernard Donna, CSJ. Washington: The Catholic University of America Press, 1964. The Fathers of the Church, Vol. 51.

On the Lord's Prayer, translated by Roy J. Deferrari, in Saint Cyprian: Treatises. New York: Fathers of the Church, Inc., 1958, Vol. 36, pp. 125-162.

Scripture Testimonies Against the Jews, Addressed to Quirinius, III, 26, in The Treatises of St. Cyprian. Oxford: J. H. Parker, 1936. A Library of the Fathers of the Holy Catholic Church, Vol. III.

On the Unity of the Catholic Church, translated by Maurice Bevenot, S.J. Westminster, Md.: Newman Press, 1957. Ancient Christian Writers.

Cyril of Jerusalem

The Catechetical Lectures of St. Cyril, translated by R. W. Church, with notes and indices. Oxford: J.H. Parker, 1838.

Lectures on the Christian Sacraments; The Procatechesis and the Five Mystagogical Catecheses, edited by F. L. Cross. London: SPCK, 1951.

The Works of St. Cyril of Jerusalem: Procatechesis and Catecheses 1-12, and Catechesis 13-18 and Mystagogical Lectures, translated by Leo P. McCauley, S.J., and Anthony A. Stephenson. Washington: The Catholic University of America Press, 1968. The Fathers of the Church, Vols. 61 and 64.

Commodianus

The Writings of Quintus Septimus Florens Tertullianus, translated by Rev. S. Thelwall and others. Edinburgh: T. and T. Clark, 1869-70. Vol. 3 includes the extant works of Commodianus.

The Didache

The Doctrine of the Twelve Apostles, translated by Charles Begg. London: SPCK; New York: E. and J.B. Young, 1898.

The Teaching of the Twelve Apostles, with facsimile text, translated by J. Rendel Harris. Baltimore: Publication Agency of the Johns Hopkins University; London: C.J. Clay, 1887.

Teaching of the Twelve Apostles, translation and commentary by Robert A. Kraft. New York: Nelson, 1965.

Egeria

Egeria's Travels, translated by John Wilkinson. London: SPCK, 1971.

The Pilgrimage of Egeria (Peregrinatio Aegeriae), translated by M.L. McClure and C.L. Feltoe. London: SPCK; New York: MacMillan,1919.

Gregory of Nyssa

The Lord's Prayer. The Beatitudes. Translated and annotated by Hilda Graef. Westminster, Md.: Newman Press, 1954.

Hippolytus

The Apostolic Tradition, translated with introduction and notes by Burton Scott Easton. Hamden, Conn.: Archon Books, 1962.

The Treatise on the Apostolic Tradition of St. Hippolytus of Rome, edited by Gregory Dix, 2nd edition. London: SPCK, 1968. Contains the Greek, Latin, and English texts.

Irenaeus

Adversus Haereses (Against the Heresies), translated and annotated by F. R. Montgomery Hitchcock. London: SPCK, 1916. Early Christian Classics.

John Cassian

The Conferences of John Cassian (1-24), translated by Edgar C.S. Gibson, M.A. New York: The Christian Literature Company, 1894. A Select Library of the Nicene and Post-Nicene Fathers of the Christian Church, second edition, Vol. 11.

John Chrysostom

Catecheses, translated and annotated by Paul W. Haskins. Westminster, Md.: Newman Press, 1963. Ancient Christian Writers, Vol. 31.

The Epistle to the Romans (Homilies on Romans), edited by Philip Schaff. New York: Charles Scribner's Sons, 1899. A Select Library of the Nicene and Post-Nicene Fathers of the Christian Church, Vol. 11.

Justin, Martyr

The Works Now Extant of St. Justin the Martyr, translated by G.J. Davie. Oxford: J.H. Parker, 1861. A Library of the Fathers of the Holy Catholic Church.

The Writings of Justin Martyr and Athenagoras, translated by Marcus Dods, George Reith, and B.P. Pratten. Edinburgh: T. and T. Clark, 1876. Ante-Nicene Christian Library, Vol. 2.

Methodius

Symposium, A Treatise on Chastity, translated by Herbert Mursurillo. Westminster, Md.: Newman Press, 1958. Ancient Christian Writers, Vol. 27.

Origen

Contra Celsum (Against Celsus), translated with an introduction and notes by Henry Chadwick. Cambridge: Cambridge University Press, 1956.

Homélies sur Jérémie (In Jeremia Homiliae), French translation by Pierre Husson, Pierre Nautin. Paris: Editions du Cerf, 1976. Sources chrétiennes (SC) n. 232.

Homélies sur les Nombres (Homily On Numbers), introduction and French translation by André Mehat. Paris: Editions du Cerf, 1951.

Homilia in Numeros and *Homilia in Jesu Nave. Patrologia Graeca,* edited by P.J. Migne, Vol. 12.

The Writings of Origen, translated by Rev. Frederick Combie. Edinburgh: T. and T. Clark, 1869-72. Ante-Nicene Christian Library, Vol. 23.

Peter Chrysologus

Much of Peter Chrysologus' writings are available only in Latin. See *Patrologia Cursum Completus Latina,* edited by J.P. Migne, Vol. 52.

Collectio Sermonum, Turnholti, Brepols, 1975- . *Corpus Christian-orum,* series Latina, Vol. 24.

Selected Sermons, translated by George E. Ganss, S.J. New York: Fathers of the Church, Inc., 1953, Vol. 17. Contains sermons on the Apostle's Creed and on the Lord's Prayer.

Pseudo-Clement

Studien zu den pseudo-Clementinen nebst Anhage: Die älteste rö-mische Bischofsliste und die pseudo-Clementinen, J. Ch. Henricks. Leipzig: 1929.

Tertullian

De Baptismo (Homily on Baptism), text edited with an introduction, translation, and commentary by Ernest Evans. London: SPCK, 1964.

De paenitentia (Treatises on Penance), On Penitence and *On Purity,* translated and annotated by William P. LeSaint, S.J. Westminster, Md.: Newman Press, 1959. Ancient Christian Writers, Vol. 28.

De praescriptione haereticorum (Prescription Against Heretics), in *The Writings of Tertullian,* Vol. 2, edited by Rev. Alexander Roberts and James Donaldson. Edinburgh: T. and T. Clark, 1852. Ante-Nicene Christian Library, Vol. 15.

Theodore of Mopsuestia

Catechetical Homilies 11-16, Commentary of Theodore of Mopsuestia on the Lord's Prayer, and on the sacraments of Baptism and the Eucharist. Cambridge: W. Heffer and Sons, Ltd., 1933. Woodbrook Studies, Vol. VI.

Commentary on the Nicene Creed (The Catechetical Homilies 1-10), edited with a critical apparatus by A. Mingana. Cambridge: W. Heffer and Sons, Ltd., 1932. The Woodbrook Studies, Vol. V.

The Eucharistic Doctrine and Liturgy of the Mystagogical Catecheses of Theodore of Mopsuestia, by Francis J. Reine. Washington: The Catholic University of America Press, 1942.

Les homélies catéchétiques de Théodore de Mopsueste (The Complete Catechetical Homilies, 1-16), translated into French by Raymond Tonneau, O.P. Vatican: Biblioteca Apostolica Vaticana, 1949. *Studi e Testi.*

Secondary Sources

The following sources are referred to throughout the course of this study:

Dictionnaire d'archéologie chrétienne et de liturgie (DACL), edited by Fernand Cabrol. Paris: Letouzey et Ané , 1913-1953.

Dictionnaire de spiritualité (DS), edited by Marcel Viller, S.J. Paris: Beauchesne et ses fils, 1937-.

Dictionnaire de théologie catholique (DTC), edited by A. Vacant and E. Mangenot. Paris: Letouzey et Ané, 1903-.

Gregorianum. Roma: Pontificia Universitas Gregoriana.

Recherches de science religieuse (RSR). Paris: Desclée de Brouwer.

Revue d'histoire ecclésiastique. Louvain: Université Catholique de Louvain, 1900-.

Sources chrétiennes. (SC), collection edited by H. de Lubac and J. Danielou. Paris: Editions du Cerf, 1943-.

Abbreviations

AT   Apostolic Tradition of Hippolytus of Rome
DACL   Dictionnaire d'archéologie chrétienne et de
        liturgie
DS   Dictionnaire de spiritualité
DTC   Dictionnaire de théologie catholique
PG   Patrologia Graeca
PL   Patrologia Latina
RHE   Revue d'histoire ecclésiastique
RSR   Recherches de science religieuse
SC   Sources chrétiennes
SPCK   Society for Promoting Christian Knowledge

Foreword

THERE is a growing realization that the revised *Rite of Christian Initiation of Adults* (RCIA) is the most far-reaching and ambitious of all the post-Vatican liturgical reforms. Liturgists, long concerned about the disintegrated unity of the sacraments of initiation when celebrated with children, welcome the restored sacramental unity of Baptism, Confirmation, and First Eucharist. Catechists are fascinated by the multi-dimensional catechesis of the catechumenate (instructional, liturgical, apostolic, communal) which can serve as a model or paradigm for all efforts of religious education, be this a post-baptismal catechumenate we call the religious education of children or programs directed towards sustaining the faith of adults already fully initiated into the Church. Sacramental theologians are taken with the insight that adult initiation is theologically normative; Christian initiation of children is a pastoral adaptation which for a long time has been in search of a proper theology. Alert pastors quickly recognize the vision of a believing Church to which the RCIA calls us.

Providentially, the appearance of the new Rite dovetails with other developments which bring home more forcefully the relevance of the RCIA as an instrument of radical Church renewal not confined to so-called mission countries. The apostolic exhortation of Paul VI, *Evangelization in the Modern World* (1975), and John Paul II's first encyclical *Redeemer of Humankind* (1979) challenge us to a more intensified preaching of the

Gospel. Statistics projecting upwards to 80 million unchurched Americans seem to bear out this very real pastoral need.

But where to begin? How to implement the RCIA? Similar to the permanent diaconate in this respect, the RCIA is not simply the revision of an already existing rite or practice, but is rather the restoration of a process that disappeared over a thousand years ago and needs to be adapted to the local churches of today. In other words, we have no recent experience of the adult catechumenate in the Roman Catholic life of this country to serve as a guide. Herein lies the value of Michel Dujarier's *The Rites of Christian Initiation: Historical and Pastoral Reflections,* perhaps best described as the most thorough and complete commentary on the liturgies of the RCIA.

Born in 1932 in Tours, France, Dujarier earned his doctorate in theology at the Institut Catholique in Paris in 1961 with a thesis on baptismal sponsorship in the early Church. A diocesan priest, he is presently in the service of the Archdiocese of Cotonou in the Popular Republic of Bénin in West Africa. In addition to his many pastoral responsibilities, which have for some years included the supervision of a catechumenate, he teaches at the Institut Catholique of West Africa at Abidjan and is the secretary general of the episcopal commission for catechesis and liturgy in French-speaking West Africa. The essays which make up this volume first appeared in *Le Calao,* the catechetical journal of West Africa, and in the author's course notes on the catechumenate published privately. They have been expertly translated and edited by Fr. Kevin Hart.

Dujarier applies a sound methodology to the rites of

Christian initiation: an *historical overview* drawn from patristic texts and liturgical sources; the anthropological and theological *meaning* of the given liturgy; the *structure* as provided in the new rite; and further *pastoral suggestions* based on his own experience, especially with the Mossi tribe. A study of this scope would only be possible from the hands of one who is not only a talented academician, but who has also actually celebrated these liturgies.

It was in June 1978 at Senanque, France, during a symposium on Christian initiation called together by Dr. Christiane Brusselmans and sponsored by W. H. Sadlier that I first met Michel Dujarier and the publication of this book became a dream. Who among the participants will ever forget the clear, enthusiastic presentations in his native French so evocative and spellbinding they could be understood in any language? Who was not moved by his gentle simplicity of spirit warmly reminiscent of the late John Paul I? It is a privilege to introduce to the English-speaking world a study which represents the life's work and ministry of one of the most inspiring Christians I know. Please God it may serve to guide us in the restoration of what could be the very future of the Church.

Rev. Charles W. Gusmer
Darlington Seminary

Introduction

The Origins of the New Rite of Christian Initiation of Adults

THE publication of the *Rite of Christian Initiation of Adults*, (hereafter referred to as the *RCIA*) on January 6, 1972, in Rome, brought to completion a work that was ten years in the making.

Even before the opening session of the Second Vatican Council, a Roman decree of April 16, 1962 authorized the restoration of the stages of the catechumenate, "by which, at appropriate intervals, and in keeping with the development of their catechetical formation, adult catechumens proceed toward the reception of Baptism, so as to sanctify their catechetical formation by sacred rites" (cf. *Maison-Dieu*, n. 71).

In reviving this ancient practice of the Church, the decree of 1962 correctly emphasized that the catechumenate is a journey towards Baptism, a journey which passes through a number of successive stages, where the process of conversion is aided and marked by liturgical rites. But unfortunately, the seven stages proposed by the Decree were simply lifted straight from the old rite.

The fathers of the Second Vatican Council were not content with this kind of restoration of the catechumenate. Instead, they specified the direction of the catechumenal journey, oriented towards the Eucharist (cf. *Decree on the Ministry and Life of Priests*, 5). Above all, the Council described the periods and thresholds of this progressive journey, insisting that they furnish the catechumenate with a genuine experience of *initiation* (cf. *Decree on the Church's Missionary Activity*, 13, 14). The Council also called for a revision of the Rite which would reflect the different stages in the initiation process and respect the tradition of the Church as well as the customs and practices of different cultures and civilizations.

The Sacred Congregation for Divine Worship undertook the task of bringing the Council's vision of Christian initiation to reality. A provisional rite was drafted and sent around the world so that local churches could experiment and send back to Rome their suggestions for revision and other advice. What we now know as the new *Rite of Christian Initiation of Adults* is the fruit of this exchange and dialogue carried out within the Church for a number of years.

Contents of the Rite

Besides being a collection of liturgical rites to mark the various stages in the process of conversion, the new Rite also contains preliminary notes which are indispensable for discovering the basic pastoral principles governing the application of the new Rite.

In addition to the normal rite of the Catechumenate Received in Stages (Chapter 1), the new Rite contains special chapters dealing with the application of the Rite of Initiation to certain pastoral situations which, up until this restoration, have not been sufficiently studied or recognized. These chapters are:

— A simplified rite (Chapter 2), and the rite to be used in danger of death (Chapter 3).
— The preparation of baptized but uncatechized adults for Confirmation and Eucharist (Chapter 4). Even though these adults have

been baptized, they, like the catechumens, need to experience a progression in faith marked and sanctified by liturgical actions.

— The new rite of Initiation of Children of Catechetical Age (Chapter 5) reflects an awareness of the psychology of school age children.

— Chapter 6 offers a selection of formulas, prayers, and texts appropriate for the celebration of the initiation of adults.

In this introductory chapter, we will consider first the structure of Christian Initiation as described in the Introduction to the RCIA. We will then offer some reflections and suggestions for implementing the Rite.

The Structure of the Initiation of Adults

ALL growth is progressive: it takes time, and passes through a number of clearly recognized stages. As a formative process by which an individual is introduced to the Christian life in all its fullness, catechumenal initiation cannot escape this dynamic law of human growth. It is important, then, to specify the different *times*, *periods*, and *stages* which mark the path of the catechumenal journey.

The RCIA distinguishes four *periods* in the spiritual growth of the prospective convert. These four periods are set apart by three principal liturgical *stages (RCIA, 6–7)*. Note that in the RCIA the term "stage" is not applied, as it was formerly, to each of the seven catechumenal rites, but is reserved for the three major liturgical rites which mark the passage of the catechumen from one period into another.

What, then, are these four *periods* and three *stages* which both distinguish and join them? The schema on page 22 may be of help to the reader as we study each of the four periods and the stage to which each period leads.

	First Period	First Stage	Second Period*	Second Stage	Third Period	Third Stage	Fourth Period
Nature	Time of the evangelization and pre-catechumenate [Awakening of Faith]	Entrance into the Catechumenate	Time of the Catechumenate [Education of Faith]	Rite of Election or Inscription of Names	Time of purification and enlightenment, or time of the baptismal retreat [Consecration of Faith]	Reception of the Sacraments of Initiation	Time of post-baptismal catechesis, or mystagogia [Deepening of Faith]
Length	Unlimited		From one to several years		Lent		Weeks of the Easter Season
Significance	First proclamation of Jesus Christ to awaken faith (Initial conversion)	First welcome into the Church	Experience of the total Christian life	Admission to the Sacraments of Initiation	Immediate and intensive preparation for the reception of the Sacraments of Initiation	Rebirth, inaugurating the life of the baptized	Deepening of sacramental experience and life in the Church
Name of the Subject	Sympathizers or Inquirers		Catechumens		The Elect		Neophytes

*For pastoral reasons, these time spans are adaptable, depending on your local situation.

Implementation of the New Rite: Guiding Principles

BEFORE going into some detail about how to implement the new Rite, we should be aware of the four general principles which should govern all serious efforts to implement the RCIA on the local level.

First of all, the new Rite is not a recipe book to be followed to the letter; rather, it is meant as a guide which of necessity demands creative adaptation if it is to be followed in spirit. We have already mentioned that it is indispensable to become familiar with the prefatory notes contained in the Introduction to the new Rite, where the general principles which underlie all the rites are enunciated. Unless the spirit of the new Rite is appreciated, all the efforts by pastors and catechists charged with its implementation will be built on sand. While this is true for implementation of the Rite in general, it is even more crucial when the condition of a particular culture or age group makes adaptation particularly necessary. Some of these adaptations require the consensus of national conferences of bishops; others can be decided by individual bishops, or by the local parish ministers (*RCIA* 64-67).

Secondly, the RCIA develops a vision of the catechumenate as a *gradual* initiation which involves not just the catechumens, sponsors, catechists, and priests, but the entire local Christian community. The process of initiation is much more than just the celebration of a number of rites, but an integral formation in all the aspects of Christian life. As with all human growth, this formation is progressive and continues over an extended period of time, as reflected in the *Decree on the Missionary Activity of the Church* (13, 14) of the Second Vatican Council.

Thirdly, the RCIA respects the dynamics of the conversion process and presupposes a close relationship between catechesis and liturgy. As emphasized in the Decree of April 16, 1972 restoring the stages of the catechumenate, the celebration of the rites of initiation, as demanded by their very nature, must correspond to the successive stages of Christian formation. In other words, the celebration of liturgical stages must parallel the successive stages of faith development.

Catechesis, like the liturgical stages, must be progressive, and the two must always go together. In the final analysis, what determines the progress of the catechumens is neither the program of catechesis nor the celebration of liturgical rites, but the faith development of the catechumen—that is, conversion.

Finally, the practical value of the new Rite will depend on the degree to which the various stages or thresholds of the conversion process are taken seriously, both by the candidates themselves and by those responsible for their formation. On this point, the history of the catechumenate in the early centuries of the Church is very revealing. The golden age of the catechumenate lasted only as long as the Church demanded of the candidates a real conversion and a sincere decision to follow Christ before they could be admitted. Once this necessary requirement was relaxed, and the Church admitted to the catechumenate those whose conversion was nominal or nonexistent, the catechumenate entered its long period of decline.

This decline of the catechumenate went hand in hand with a general weakening of the commitment and life-style characteristic of the early Church.

We cannot, then, emphasize enough that the revitalization of Christian initiation is directly dependent (1) on the restoration of the two essential stages of the initiation process: entrance into the catechumenate and the election of the candidates to proceed toward Baptism; and (2) on the seriousness with which the community will judge the worthiness of the candidates to proceed to these two stages.

The Awakening of Faith

If the purpose of the first *period* of the initiation process (designated as the period of precatechumenate) is to bring the inquirers to the initial conversion essential for entrance into the catechumenate (the first *stage* or *threshold* in the initiation process), what are the conditions and circumstances necessary to generate this conversion?

The dialogue between the minister and the candidate presented for entrance into the Catechumenate (*RCIA* 75-81, 370-371) clarifies the essential character of initial conversion: belief in the living God and in Christ the Savior, and some external manifestation of the beginning of an interior spiritual life. It is an awareness of this essential character which should guide one's efforts in fostering its realization in the candidates.

To achieve this kind of conversion, it is obvious, then, that the candidates must have the opportunity to reflect on their deepest aspirations, to discover Christ as the Way, the Truth, and the Life, and to experience some kind of relationship with God and with the ecclesial community. If we consider this reflection and discovery of Christ and Church to be the "content" of this period, we must also realize that this "content" is both intimately personal and unique for each candidate. There is no question here of structuring a program which could then be followed by the candidates, either individually or as a group. The precatechumenal period must be tailored to each individual inquirer. Remember, this is not so much a time for learning or instruction as it is a gradual time of personal reflection, search, discovery, and response. Of all the periods and stages of the initiation process, the precatechumenate is the most difficult to implement, precisely because it is so personal. It is also, perhaps, the most important, for it is the foundation or starting point so determinative of the entire catechumenal journey.

The realization of an effective period of precatechumenate will demand our most concerted efforts, mindful of the indispensable role of the Christian community in awakening and sustaining the faith of the inquirers.

As proposed in the RCIA, the stage of entrance into the catechumenate requires more articulation on the part of the candidate than any of the other stages. But the sincerity and depth of this articulation depends on the sincerity and depth of the initial conversion to Christ and the willingness to follow Him, which cannot develop without a period of extended reflection and personal search.

Education of Faith

The four components of Christian education characteristic of the period of the catechumenate properly speaking are: catechetical instruction, exposure to the Christian life, participation in liturgical rites, and an introduction to the apostolic life of the Church. The following principles may guide us in this four-fold educational endeavor:

1. *Christian education must become more experiential and less instructional.*

   Unfortunately, catechumens are often considered to be "students," both from the point of view of what they are expected to "learn" as well as to how they are "taught."

   After so many years of "convert classes," it will take a while for this image to disappear—which makes it all the more urgent that we discover ways in which to organize educational groups marked by a spirit of sharing and lively exchange, instead of students seated at the feet of a master.

2. *Christian education involves the entire Christian community.*

   Involving the entire Christian community means more than just informing them of the existence and progress of the catechumenal groups. They should also be encouraged to participate in the catechumenal liturgies, thereby demonstrating that the entire community shares in the responsibility of sponsorship, as well as in discerning the worthiness of the candidates presented for admission to the catechumenate and the Sacraments of Initiation.

3. *Personal and communal prayer experiences play a vital role in Christian education.*

   Catechesis on prayer should present the catechumens with an opportunity to reflect together and share what they experienced in a previous prayer celebration, rather than try to design celebrations whose purpose is to illustrate a *particular* aspect of previous instruction.

4. *Implementation of the Rites of Transition in the course of the catechumenate period is indispensable.*

While the new Rite indicates that it is *possible* to celebrate the rites of the presentations as rites of transition (*RCIA* 53) during the time of the catechumenate, from a pastoral and psychological standpoint, their celebration is really *necessary*. Since this long period of growth must be marked and sustained by the passage of a number of intervening levels, it seems both pointless and even harmful to reserve the celebration of the rites of transition either to the very beginning or the very end of the catechumenate period.

Consecreation and Deepening of Faith

If the period of the catechumenate proper is one of growth and education in faith, it is in the period of purification and enlightenment that this growth is both clearly manifested and deepened. During the Lenten season the entire Church—not just the elect— lives most clearly the paschal mystery and renews its own conversion to Christ. For that reason, then, the Church can in turn support the elect by her prayer and lead them by her example.

But this kind of prayerful, supportive, and exemplary community is possible during the Lenten period of enlightenment *only* if it has also manifested itself as such before. If not, then even an intense period of enlightenment and beautiful liturgical celebrations will amount to nothing more than a short-lived and superficial show.

Likewise, if initiation through Baptism is to be properly understood as not just the culmination of a previous period of preparation but also as a commitment to grow in faith in the future, then the Christian community must continue to journey with and support the neophytes throughout the period of post-baptismal catechesis, and beyond. Even the most beautiful and moving Easter liturgies can have very short-lived results if the catechumenate remains somehow separated from the full Christian community. When the neophytes feel they are not welcomed by a loving and supportive community of believers, they may find themselves surrounded by a sea of anonymous faces.

In any case, there will be no renewal of the catechumenate without a simultaneous renewal of evangelization, announcing the message of salvation in Christ to those who have yet to hear his name, and a deepening of its meaning and acceptance among those who have.

Whether or not we are ready to begin implementation of the RCIA, it is an invitation to widen our perspectives of what it means to be and live the Christian life.

Chapter 1
The Rite of Entrance into the Catechumenate

CHRISTIAN initiation begins with the stage of inquiry or precatechumenate, a time of intimate and personal discovery of Christ as savior, and a willingness to embark on a journey of faith in order to deepen one's knowledge, experience, and love of the Lord. This is what we call *initial conversion*.

With this experience of initial conversion, the candidates can approach the first threshold of their journey of faith: entrance into the catechumenate. In this chapter we will look at this first liturgical stage of the new Rite under four aspects: its history, its meaning, and its structure in the revised Rite; finally, we will reflect on some of the pastoral experiences of its implementation.

Historical Overview

The Catechumenal Journey

As we mentioned earlier, the Church has always recognized two clearly distinguishable periods in the journey of initiation, each of which leads the candidate to a new threshold. The first of these periods is that of inquiry, or precatechumenate. It begins not in church, but within a family, at work, at a meeting or gathering place, when the Good News of Christ is heard — *really* heard — for the first time. It begins not with a sermon, but with a few words shared by a Christian member of the family, a co-worker, a friend, or even a stranger.

Origen of Alexandria describes the manner in which the precatechumenate was carried out in the early part of the third century when he says, "The Christians began by testing the souls of those who would listen to them, and then took them aside privately for instruction."[1] Origen also notes that this initial conversion had to be supported by a visible change in the person's life: "Before they are allowed to join with the community, they must give sufficient evidence of their desire to live a virtuous life."[2] Only then could they be officially welcomed into the Church.

The stage to which initial conversion leads is termed "Entrance into the Catechumenate"; in reality it is nothing less than entrance into the Church. It is after this initial evangelization and conversion that the "convert" becomes a "Christian."

While the term "catechumenate" is often used

today in speaking of the entire initiation process, in the strict sense (which we will be using) "catechumenate" designates the *second period* of the initiation process. At the end of this period, those who "have demonstrated to the best of their ability to desire only those things which are fitting for the life of a Christian,"[3] and who "are convinced of and sincerely believe all that we have taught and said, and who are able to live by it"[4] will advance to the third period, immediate preparation for Baptism. This immediate preparation leads to the third and final stage, the reception of the Sacraments of Initiation, which makes the Christian a full member of the faithful.

Origen explains the significance of these two periods and stages by drawing on the image of the Exodus. For him, the inquirers' decision to leave their pagan beliefs behind them and enter into the Catechumenate is comparable to the flight of the Israelites from Egypt and their passage through the Red Sea. Similarly, the significance of Baptism is symbolized by the crossing of the River Jordan by the Israelites and their entrance into the promised land, after having undergone their desert experience, during which they received the law and accepted it as a way of life.

The early Fathers applied yet another image to the catechumenal journey we have described thus far: the image of the gestation period of an infant in the mother's womb. Accordingly, entrance into the catechumenate is a type of conception, in which the catechumen is implanted into the womb of the Church. Baptism is, then, a new birth which comes about only after a necessary period of formation.[5]

Entrance into the Catechumenate: Historical Overview

The earliest historical evidence of the rite of entrance into the catechumenate comes to us through Hippolytus of Rome (third century). In particular, Hippolytus emphasizes the conditions governing entrance into the catechumenate. The candidates were closely examined as to their readiness to enter the Church in order that they may listen to the Word. For this examination, the community relied heavily on the testimony of those whom we call (today) "sponsors," the people who were responsible for evangelizing and forming the candidates. Note that this examination was part of the rite of entrance, and consisted of (1) a dialogue between the "doctors" (teachers), the candidates, and their sponsors; and (2) a catechesis on the fundamentals of Christian life.

Hippolytus also mentions a "welcome of the candidates into the community," which was celebrated with the entire Christian community. This welcome, in effect, gave the new catechumens the right to join with the community and participate in the catechesis which took place during the Liturgy of the Word.

Origen mentions these same conditions of examination and welcome, but also adds a third: the candidates must renounce their former idols so as to faithfully follow Christ.

In the fourth, fifth, and sixth centuries, these three fundamental aspects of the rite of entrance into the catechumenate continued to be endorsed, but they are accompanied by a number of additional rituals. St. Augustine specifies that converts must express their faith before they can be admitted to the Church. "After this instruction (i.e.: pre-catechesis), the candidate is asked if he believes these truths, and if he is willing to conform his life to them. Once he has responded 'yes', he is, according to the rite, to be signed with the cross and dealt with in accordance with the custom of the Church."[6]

During these early centuries, there were a number of liturgical rites which accompanied the examination of the candidates and their renunciation of former idols. We mention here four of these rites, noting that their use varied widely according to local custom and circumstances.

The most essential of these rites, and the only one which was used universally, is the rite of signation: the sign of the cross made on the forehead of each candidate. Certain scholars question whether in some parts of Northern Africa the sign of the cross was done in the form of an indelible tattoo.[7] This rite expressed that the candidates belonged henceforth to Christ, whose sign they wear and whose name they bear: "Christian." In making this sign of the cross, the minister prayed that the catechumens would carry in their hearts the sign of Christ made on their foreheads.[8] Because of a misinterpretation of the formula used at the signation, *"Accipe signum crucis tam in fronte quam in corde,"* the sign of the cross came to be administered on the forehead *and* over the heart. This redundant signation eventually gave rise to the practice of the Church in Gaul in which other parts of the body, in addition to the forehead and chest, were marked with the sign of the cross.

Another liturgical rite which sometimes accompanied the candidates' entrance into the catechumenate was the imposition of hands. In most cases the imposition of hands was tied to the rite of signation and welcome by the community. It signified that the candidates were now under the care of the Church. But since this gesture was repeated after every meeting of the catechumens, it is possible that it was also seen as a rite of exorcism.[9]

The churches of Northern Africa developed the custom of giving salt to the new catechumens,[10] and this rite was also part of the Roman practice from the beginning of the sixth century. The significance of this rite is essentially one of hospitality and welcome, with an allusion to the Passover meal. Others also see in this rite a symbol of purification and wisdom.

Finally, we must mention the rite of breathing on the candidates, to "blow away" any evil spirits. However, we find scant historical evidence for this rite.[11]

Unfortunately, the time came when these rites of entrance into the catechumenate were celebrated even'though there was no verification of the faith of the candidates through examination of the witnesses and sponsors, and no profession of faith by the candidates. This marks the beginning of the decline of the catechumenate. It is crucial, then, in our attempts to restore the catechumenate, that we give to this period of precatechumenate formation and conversion the serious attention it demands. Entrance into the Catechumenate must be marked by discernment, an authentic adhesion in faith to Christ, a sincere decision to follow him and live according to his Word, and a renunciation of all unChristian attitudes and practices.

The Meaning of the Rite of Entrance into the Catechumenate

ENTRANCE into the catechumenate is the first liturgical threshold to be crossed in one's journey of initiation. It is, then, a solemn recognition and consecration of the search and discernment which are the essential characteristics of the period of precatechumenate and initial evangelization.

The Rite of Entrance is the first official encounter between the Church and the candidate who has undergone an initial conversion. On the candidate's part, it manifests a desire to follow Christ. This includes a willingness not only to pursue the discovery of Jesus but also to conform one's life to the Gospel and to renounce all former unchristian practices. On her part, the Church, through the symbolism of the liturgical rite, welcomes the convert into the People of God, and in so doing, gives added impetus to the process of full conversion and progressive initiation. Entrance into the catechumenate is nothing less than entrance into the Church, whereby the "convert" becomes "Christian." Later on, Baptism will transform the "Christian" into a "member of the faithful," but the action of God's transforming grace is already present as the candidate enters the catechumenate.

The RCIA specifies that only those who have experienced an initial but genuine conversion may cross the threshold into the catechumenate (RCIA, 15-16). Since faith in itself is not visible, the candidates must be able to give some clearly recognizable exterior signs of their nascent faith. These exterior signs of faith can be grouped under three categories.

First, the candidates must provide the signs of the beginning of an authentic spiritual life. Such signs would include a willingness to change their life and enter into relationship with God through Christ, an initial sense of repentance, the beginning of a prayer-life, and lived experience with the Christian community and spirit.

Secondly, the candidates must afford some grasp of the essential Christian doctrines of faith in the one, true, and living God, and in Jesus Christ as savior, as well as some understanding of what the Church is.

A third sign which the candidates must furnish is that they be presented and supported by sponsors, who, after assisting the candidates in their personal search and discovery of Christ, can attest to their faith, to their willingness to grow in that faith, and to their behavior.

The RCIA also points out that Entrance into the catechumenate should not take place too soon after a candidate's initial conversion or the beginning of the search and discovery of Christ (RCIA, 50). It takes time for this initial faith to grow and to begin to manifest the first essential exterior signs of true conversion. Moreover, it is hoped that a given community will not celebrate the rite of entrance too often, in order to keep its solemn and communal character. Once, or twice, a year would seem sufficient.

The Structure of the Rite of Entrance into the Catechumenate

RECALL that Entrance into the Catechumenate marks one's entrance into the Church. Consequently, it is preferable that this rite be celebrated in the presence of the entire community, or at least a part of the community, including friends and relatives of the candidates, as well as catechists and priests (*RCIA*, 70).

Also necessary would be the presence of the sponsors, who present the candidates to the Church (*RCIA*, 71) and who will continue to assist them in their discovery of the Christian way of life.

The Rite of Entrance into the Catechumenate consists of two parts: the reception of the candidates and the Liturgy of the Word. The Rite may be followed by celebration of the Eucharist.

Reception of the Candidates: The Rite can be celebrated either before the doors of the church, at an appropriate place within the church or even at a place other than the church if this would be preferable.

Opening Dialogue: The celebrant greets the candidates and invites them, along with their sponsors, to step forward (*RCIA*, 74). He then asks the candidates their names, or even better, he calls them by name. In the dialogue which then follows (and the more spontaneous the better) he asks them what they are looking for (*RCIA*, 75).

First Promise: Adapting his words to the responses given by the candidates, the celebrant then explains to the candidates (again, the more spontaneous the better) the journey of faith which they are undertaking, a journey in which Christ will lead them by his love to eternal life (*RCIA,* 76). He then asks the candidates if they are ready to embark on this journey, following the leadership of Christ. He also asks the sponsors if they are equally ready to assist the candidates in their discovery of Christ and to follow him (*RCIA,* 77).

If the local religious customs and practices would seem to warrant it, an exorcism and a renunciation of false gods would follow the first promise of the candidates and sponsors. The Rite gives Episcopal Conferences the right to adapt the formulas for this exorcism and renunciation according to local needs and circumstances (*RCIA,* 78-82).

Liturgical Gestures: The signation follows immediately. While the celebrant alone pronounces the words (*RCIA,* 82-83), the catechists and sponsors may trace the cross on the forehead and the senses if the candidates are numerous. If circumstances demand, the signation of the different senses can be omitted in part or in whole (*RCIA,* 83-87).

In areas where non-Christian religions give a new name to those who become members, the Conference of Bishops may decide that the catechumens may receive at the Rite of Entrance a Christian name or a name familiar in their culture, provided that it has a Christian meaning. If the new name is not given here, it will be given on Holy Saturday.

Welcome into the Church: Certain local customs may

be used to express entrance into the community, such as the giving of salt or the presentation of a cross or medal. The Conference of Bishops may permit the use of these customs in the Rite of Entrance, and these may take place either before or after the celebrant invites the catechumens and their sponsors to enter into the church or other suitable place (*RCIA*, 90).

The Liturgy of the Word

The Liturgy of the Word takes place inside the church or other suitable place. It includes readings from the Scripture and time for prayer.

The liturgy begins with a brief address by the celebrant to the catechumens in order to impress upon them the dignity of the Word of God proclaimed and heard in the Church. The book of the Scriptures is then carried in procession and placed reverently on the lectern. If deemed appropriate, the Scriptures may then be incensed (*RCIA*, 91). One or several readings appropriate for the new catechumens are then proclaimed, followed by a homily (*RCIA*, 92). At the end of the homily, the celebrant may present each of the catechumens with a book of the Gospels (*RCIA*, 93).

Then, all those assembled pray for the catechumens, that they may complete the journey they have just begun, as well as for their sponsors and for the entire community who will be supporting them. The celebrant concludes with an oration (*RCIA*, 94-95).

The celebrant then briefly reminds the catechumens that they have been welcomed with great joy into the community and exhorts them to strive to live in accordance with the Word they have listened to. The catechumens are then dismissed with their sponsors, and the Liturgy of the Eucharist may follow.

Points for Reflection

WHILE the work of translating the new Rite in the vernacular is now an accomplished fact, the task of *adapting* it to serve the needs of local communities is yet to be done. The Rite itself urges us to undertake a truly creative adaptation, an adaptation carried out in the spirit proposed by the Church.[12]

In this section we will offer several examples of these attempts at adaptation. Because these adaptations were developed in cultures and circumstances which might be foreign to many Americans and Europeans, the reader should be aware that in no way are these adaptations to be considered normative or readily applicable to his or her own cultural milieu. It is hoped that they will prompt the reader to consider and research appropriate adaptation for his or her own cultural situation.

General Problems in the Structure and Order of the Rite

The structure of the Rite of Entrance into the Catechumenate raises a question concerning the place given to the Liturgy of the Word. The new Rite places the celebration of the Word in the second part of the Rite of Entrance, after the dialogue with the catechumens and sponsors and their welcome into the community. This order seems justifiable, since one must first enter into the Church before one can receive the Word of God.

Nevertheless, one could object that this order seems to run counter to the fundamental principle of liturgy of not celebrating a rite without first situating it by the proclamation of the Scriptures. Therefore, would it not be preferable to order the Rite of Entrance into Catechumenate in the following manner? Begin, as the rite suggests, with the dialogue and welcoming into the church, but place the promise to follow Christ and the rite of signation after the Liturgy of the Word. This would give us a liturgical celebration with three parts:

— *Welcome of the candidates*. This would be done at the entrance to the church, and would include the presentation or calling of the candidates; the dialogue between celebrant, candidates, and sponsors; and entry into the church, and welcoming by the community.
— *Celebration of the Word*. Includes the procession and veneration of the Scriptures, the readings, and the homily.
— *The first promise and the rite of becoming Christian*. This would include the renunciation of unChristian religious practices, with an exorcism and promise of fidelity to Christ in the journey of faith; the primary liturgical rite of signation; and the secondary rites— giving of a new name, presentation of a cross, presentation of the Gospels.

Where the Rite is Celebrated

The new rite gives great liberty concerning the place in which Entrance into the Catechumenate can be celebrated. The principle which should guide our selection of place is this: whatever will make the Rite of Entrance as expressive as possible.

The first part of the rite could be done outside, in order to highlight the procession by which the candidates and sponsors enter the church. Yet this procedure would make it difficult for the community waiting inside to participate in the important dialogue with which the rite begins.

One solution would be to carry out the first part of the Rite inside the church, but towards the back. This would also preserve the means for highlighting the procession of entrance into the church.

Some might prefer to conduct the entire rite of Entrance in the Catechumenate *outside,* in a large open space. When celebrated outside, care should be taken to preserve two easily distinguishable spaces: the place of the community (analagous to the recreation room of a home where the family gathers), and the place for the candidates and sponsors (analagous to a vestibule or parlor where guests or strangers are first received).

The Time of the Celebration

In order to facilitate the participation of the community, as the new Rite recommends, the Entrance into the Catechumenate is often celebrated during a Sunday Mass. But in many large or urban parishes, the crowd and the schedule of Masses do not always assure an atmosphere of calm, or enough time necessary for this important ceremony. It might, then, be preferable to conduct the ceremony in the evening. Often, an evening liturgy, beginning just before sunset or at twilight, assures an atmosphere of meditation and calm, particularly when the ceremony is held outside. The advantages of celebrating at this time of day is already recognized in the scheduling of Holy Week services. Since many parishes already schedule Sunday Masses on Saturday evenings, the Entrance into the Catechumenate might be effectively celebrated at the last Saturday evening Mass.

The Assembly and the Ministers

Modern churches with moveable chairs offer great possibilities for the setting of this celebration. The entire Christian community, including those baptized as well as those who are already catechumens, could assemble, seated on chairs arranged in a large semicircle on either side of the celebrant's chair, with all facing the entrance of the church. The candidates would be waiting outside, facing the assembly and celebrant, waiting to cross the threshold of the church, to come inside and be incorporated into the community.

The ministers of the Rite of Entrance include the priest, head of the community, who presides over the celebration, and assisting ministers (priests and deacons). It is also important that those who are responsible for the direction of the catechumenate as well as other parish and community groups are represented in the ceremony. The latter's presence is important because they exercise a specific role in the celebration, particularly in the presentation of the candidates, and in the community's expression of welcome to the new catechumens. For example, these representatives may come as a group before the celebrant, and one of them announce (as much as possible in his own words) to the celebrant and the community the candidates' desire to enter the community. They may also take part in the dialogue or in the rites of welcome.

Finally, we must be mindful of the important role of the sponsors or godparents, who stand behind their charges, not only to testify on their behalf, but also to commit themselves to supporting them all along their journey.

Reception of the Candidates

Welcome: The new Rite suggests that the Rite of Entrance begin with the priest or deacon coming before the assembled pre-catechumens and their sponsors, and then greeting the candidates and those who are presenting them in a friendly manner (*RCIA,* 74). This way of beginning seems very brusque. It would be better if this opening appearance and greeting of the celebrant were preceded by the following:

> *A preparation of the assembly gathered inside the Church.* This community who will wel-come the new catechumens should be gath-ered not just in a physical sense, but gathered in faith. Thus it would be fitting that they first sing together and then be led in prayer by the celebrant.

> *It is not the responsibility of the celebrant to begin the dialogue.* Rather, it is the responsi-bility of one of the community representa-tives to first present the candidates to the celebrant and to report on their progress in their journey of faith. The celebrant should then respond to this representative, before

he (himself or his delegate) goes outside to greet the candidates. He then proceeds with the dialogue and the rites of welcoming. It is also desirable for the entire community, as well as the celebrant, to greet the candidates.

The call: The new Rite (75) prescribes that the celebrant asks each candidate his or her name. First of all, this is simply not polite; secondly, it suggests that the celebrant has not been a part of their formation up to this point. It seems better, then, to follow the alternative procedure suggested by the Rite (75): The celebrant calls each candidate by name, to which the candidate responds, "Present." In order to express that it is God himself, acting through the celebrant, who calls the candidates, and to express the proper interior disposition which should underlie the candidate's response, a better formulation of the response would be, "Here I am, Lord " or, "I am ready, Lord " or, "Lord, I am yours." Some prefer to defer the call of the candidates until the imposition of hands, and for this opening dialogue call the candidates by their name given at birth. In any case, it seems that a more fitting place for call of the candidates would be *after* the opening dialogue as presented in the Rite.

The dialogue: In the dialogue, the celebrant asks the candidates what they desire and why have they come. He can use the formula suggested in the Rite, but it would be better if he could conduct this dialogue in a more spontaneous manner by using his own words. The brief model outlined by the Rite concentrates on faith and eternal life, but it also suggests some alternatives: the grace of Christ, entrance into the Church, etc.

It would seem better to center the opening dialogue

on John 14, 6 ("I am the way, the truth, and the life. No one comes to the Father except through me."), which Vatican II presents as a good summary of the initial faith of the candidates [13] and which expresses the essential discovery of the pre-catechumens: Jesus is the Way who leads to the Father; we encounter him in his Church so that he can communicate to us his Truth and his Life.

The First Promise and Renunciation: This part of the rite is preceded by an invitation made by the celebrant (*RCIA*, 76). This invitation summarizes the catechesis of the candidates thus far, and closes with a question eliciting a response from the candidates to follow the leadership of Christ.

The renunciation of false worship is presented as an *option* by the Rite. There would be no need for this ceremony except in places where false worship is prevalent. In some sense this is regrettable, because no culture is without its "pagan" practices, which must be renounced by committing oneself to Christ.[14]

The RCIA suggests that the rite of breathing on the candidates, a form of exorcism, should take place before the renunciation. The rite is optional, since it might not be acceptable in certain cultures.

In effect, the renunciation states in negative terms what the promise to follow Christ does more positively. While the RCIA places the renunciation after the promise, it would seem more logical to reverse the order, as was the case in former times. The renunciation of false worship could then be seen as doing away with what would hinder one's commitment to follow Christ.

In implementing the rite, some have combined both these positive and negative dimensions into one formulation, which has the advantage of not casting the former religious beliefs and practices of the candidates in too pejorative a light. The Rite itself gives local Episcopal Conferences the right to establish more appropriate formulations (*RCIA* 80 and 371).

The Commitment of the Community: The community's commitment to the new catechumens is expressed by the question which the priest addresses to the sponsors and to all the faithful who are present — either just one question *(RCIA, 77)* or, even better, several questions *(RCIA, 81)*. It is often preferable to distinguish between these two categories of Christians responsible for supporting the catechumens. This distinction seems to highlight the responsibility of the sponsors and confirms their prophetic role in regard to their candidates.

The Signation: The signation of all the senses of the body can be an excellent expression of the need for faith to penetrate every aspect of a person's life. The Rite prescribes that multiple signation should be administered not only by the priest but also, following his lead, by the catechists or by the sponsors *(RCIA, 83)*. On the other hand, if the candidates are numerous, the celebrant may simply make one sign of the cross over all the candidates. The catechists or the sponsors could then trace this sign over the individual catechists *(RCIA, 84)*.

The order of the signations could be as follows: the forehead, the ears, the eyes, the mouth, the chest, and the shoulders, completed by the final general signation which is reserved to the celebrant.

The signation of the shoulders may prevent some difficulty, particularly in cultures where the "yoke" is not used in farming, or in cultures where heavy loads are not carried on the shoulders. In this case, a signation of the hands may be a better expression of the need to express our faith in our daily work.

Another alternative would be to have the sponsors present their candidate with a cross, to be worn around the neck or hung on a wall at home. This visible sign could serve as a reminder that they are called to be Christian wherever they go and in every aspect of their lives. The giving of a religious medal here, other than a cross, would have no essential significance and should not be considered as a viable option.

The adaptations of the Rite in the Mossi tribe of Africa furnish another acceptable option: the celebrant raises a large cross over all the candidates, just before the signation begins, while invoking the name of Jesus Christ. The cross is then raised above each candidate during the signation of the senses.

The Rites of Welcome

The rites of welcoming are particularly important for expressing the entrance of the candidates into the heart of the Church. The essential rite is, of course, the invitation of the candidates to come into the church and the solemn entrance processsion which follows immediately (*RCIA*, 90). The RCIA also permits additional rites at this point, but it is important to see these additional rites not as just subordinate but as veritable rites of welcoming. The choice of these additional rites will necessarily be conditioned by local custom and circumstances. What follows are some practical examples:

The rite of salt, a tradition in the Church, signifies

hospitality and peace. In order to distinguish this primary significance from secondary significances (purification, or preservation) or from any counter-significance (salt can be considered dangerous for a pregnant woman), large chunks of rock salt could be given. Among the Mossi tribe, each new catechumen receives a chunk of salt in his/her hands. After tasting the salt, the candidate passes it to the sponsor. This salt is used in preparing the agape meal.

The rite of water receives its significance from the oriental custom of greeting strangers at the entrance to the home. The guests were sometimes given a glass of water to drink; sometimes water was sprinkled on the threshold as a sign of welcome.

The rite of imposition of hands, a long-standing tradition in the Church, is also very expressive and may be joined to one or the other rites of welcome. The candidates process, while singing, to the celebrant who, remaining seated, rests his hands on the head of each. After an invitation to pray and a period of silence, the celebrant and the assisting priests extend their hands while the celebrant says the prayer.

The giving of a new name: Receiving a new name is of great importance in cultures where names carry a descriptive meaning, and where a new name is given to mark entrance into a new state of life. Even in cultures where the catechumen already has a Christian name, a new name, which describes some aspect of the person's life, can be given. The celebrant introduces and concludes this rite with a prayer. It would seem appropriate that it be the *sponsor,* resting his/her hands on the shoulders of the candidate, who gives the new name.

The Liturgy of the Word

The Book of the Scriptures: During this rite, the place and role of the Bible must be highlighted in order to show that the new catechumen is admitted to listen to the Word in the Church and that he or she must strive to live according to it.

The procession with the Bible, then, demands a certain solemnity. The Book of the Scriptures should be held high, with candle bearers on either side. The celebrant could incense the Bible and then hold it up for veneration by the community. This veneration may be in the form of sung acclamation, an "Exultet" in the form of a hymn of praise to the Word of God.

Presenting each candidate with a copy of the Scriptures, either after the homily or the signation, could have great significance, especially if the presentation were accompanied by a brief exhortation such as, "Hear the Word and be faithful to it."

If the candidates are illiterate, the presentation of a copy of the Scriptures could be replaced by having the candidates place their hands on the Bible or bow before it, and singing an appropriate acclamation.

The Readings: The Rite proposes Gen. 12:1-4a and John 1:35-42, with Psalm 32 as responsorial (*RCIA,* 372). Other readings may also be appropriate. Deut. 30:11-20, and Mt. 7:13-21, if one takes the theme of "the two ways." Joshua 24:1-2, 4, 16-24 or 16-28, and John 14:1-6 (adding, if desirable, 12:35-36 and 8:12) if one takes the theme of covenant, or readings from the Lectionary, #743. The readings are then followed by the homily.

Concluding Prayer: The concluding prayer is a prayer

"for the catechumens" (*RCIA*, 94). It is not, then, the catechumens who should offer the petitions, but rather the catechists, the sponsors, or those in charge of the catechumenate. If the Rite of Entrance' is not followed by a Eucharisitic Liturgy, it may be fitting to close the rite with an extended prayer of thanksgiving, somewhat like a Preface, with sung acclamations. As for the dismissal, it would be well to use one that is more developed than what is suggested in the Rite.

In closing this chapter on the Rite of Entrance into the Catechumenate, we note, once again, that the candidate who passes through this stage of the initiation process now has the status of "Christian," although not yet a "member of the faithful." He or she has been conceived in the womb of the Church, but has yet to be born.

Notes

[1] Origen, *Against Celsus,* III, 51, 2.

[2] *Ibid.,* III, 51, 3.

[3] *Ibid.*

[4] Justin, *Apology I,* 61, 2.

[5] Cf. Michel Dujarier, "Le catéchuménat et la maternité de l'Eglise," in *Maison Dieu,* 71 (1962, 3), pp. 78-93.

[6] Augustine, *First Catechetical Instruction,* XXVI, 50.

[7] Rondet, "La croix sur le front," in *RSR,* Vol. 24, 1950, p. 358. Many scholars, however, do not share his opinion.

[8] Augustine, *Sermon 107,* VI, 7.

[9] *AT,* 19; Augustine, *De peccatorum meritis,* II, 26, 42.

[10] Augustine, *First Catechetical Instruction* XXVI, 50; *Confessions, I, XI, 17.* In his *De pec. mer.* Augustine mentions that salt, or exorcised bread, was given to the catechumens throughout their period of formation.

[11] See Canon 7 of the Council of Constantinople (Cf. *Canons of the First Four General Councils: Nicaea, Constantinople, Ephesus, and Chalcedon,* ed. by Edwin Knox Mitchell, Oxford: Clarendon Press, 1880.) See also Peter Chrysologus, Bishop of Ravenna, *Sermon 52* in *PL* 52, 343.

[12] The Rite not only invites Episcopal Conferences to make the necessary adaptations for their countries, but also urges the celebrant to "use fully and intelligently the freedom which is given to him either in the General Introduction (34) or in the rubrics of the rite," (*RCIA,* 67) so as to "accommodate the rite, according to his prudent pastoral judgment, to the circumstances of the candidates and others who are present."

[13] See "Missionary Activity of the Church," Vatican Council Documents, par. 13, cited in *RCIA,* 9.

[14] Note that Hippolytus extends this renunciation to certain professions too closely associated with the three major sins of idolatry, murder, and impurity. Tertullian takes a similar stance in his treatise "On Idolatry."

Chapter 2
The Catechumenate
and Its Rites

"CATECHUMENATE" in the strict sense is the period of formation which falls between the stage of entrance into the catechumenate and the stage of election. This pastoral formation of the catechumens "continues until they have matured sufficiently in their conversion of faith. If necessary, it may last for several years" (RCIA, 98).

What are the liturgical ceremonies during this period which will sustain the journey of faith?

Catechumenal Formation in the Earliest Centuries

BECAUSE of a lack of primary historical sources, it is difficult to describe in any detail the catechumenal practice of the early Church. This lack of specific historical data is not really surprising when we consider that in the third century, prolonged catechumenal formation was so much a part of the life of the Christian community and so taken for granted that it was not the subject of special study.

Later on, in the fourth and fifth centuries, the long period of preparation so characteristic of earlier times was shortened and was more or less confined to the Lenten period. What historical evidence we do have comes mainly from this period of the Church's history, and deals more with the period of enlightenment and purification (the "baptismal retreat") than with the period of the catechumenate in the strict sense.

With these limitations in mind, let us examine what early documents we do have, and try to delineate some of the main aspects of the catechumenate period, basing our study chiefly on the *Apostolic Tradition* of Hippolytus of Rome (c. 215) and on the pastoral practices in Egypt and Palestine during the first half of the third century as they surface in the homilies of Origen.

In the *Apostolic Tradition* (18, 19) Hippolytus deals with the rites which accompany the catechesis of the catechumens during a three year period of preparation:

"When the teacher has finished the catechesis, the catechumens pray by themselves, apart from the faithful. The women, whether they be catechumens or faithful, pray in a separate place. When the catechumens have finished praying, they do not give one another the kiss of peace, for their kiss is not yet holy. The faithful greet each other, the men greeting the men, and the women greeting the other women. But the men do not greet the women. The women all cover their heads with a pallium, not just with a linen cloth since this would not be sufficient enough to veil them."

"When the prayer is finished, the teacher imposes hands over the catechumens and then dismisses them. The teacher, whether he be a cleric or a layman, should do this."

The catechesis which Hippolytus speaks of in these paragraphs should not be understood as directed just to catechumens, but rather to the entire Christian community, especially the faithful, that is, those who are already baptized.

The catechesis is accompanied by a prayer and an imposition of hands. The prayer Hippolytus speaks of is the prayer of the whole community, followed by a kiss of peace. Note that the kiss of peace is reserved to those who have received the sacraments of initiation.[1]

There then follows a special prayer for the catechumens which is offered by the catechist. It is accompanied by an imposition of hands, which most likely carried with it the significance of an exorcism.

The setting which Hippolytus describes is that of a Christian community which meets regularly, in which the catechumens have been invited to participate.

Another theologian of the third century, Origen, confirms Hippolytus' description of the structure of the catechumenate.[2] The most recent studies of Pierre Nautin[3] also shed new light on the catechumenal practice of the early Church.

The homilies of Origen show that the community gathered every day to hear the Word of God.[4] These liturgies of the Word were followed by a Eucharist only on Fridays (most likely in the evening) and on Sundays. While these liturgies were for the entire community, many Christians did not participate, except on feast days.

The liturgies of the Word took place very early in the morning, before the members began their work for the day, and often before sunrise. Both Clement of Alexandria and Hippolytus attest to this.[5] Origen gives us the format of these celebrations:[6]

— An opening prayer;
— A rather long reading from the Old Testament (The Old Testament books were read in sequence);
— A sermon by a priest (According to Hippolytus, this could be done either by a priest or a layman);
— On Sundays, the celebration included a passage from the Gospel. A reading from the Acts or from one of the Epistles was also possible, and If so, was done before the Gospel;
— A final prayer and the kiss of peace (mentioned above by Hippolytus).

Origen also relates that for the catechumens who gathered with the community, the sermon served as their catechesis. But because of the length (approximately one hour) of these celebrations, not many members of the community participated. Even among those who made the effort to come, there were some who paid little attention, some who left before the end.

Fourth and Fifth Centuries

During this period, historical data concerning the time of formation between entrance into the catechumenate and the beginning of Lent is extremely scarce. In part, this is due to the fact that the former long period of preparation was compressed into the forty days of Lent, which was more a period of retreat and spiritual reflection than a period of catechetical formation. Only one text, that of Augustine in his treatise "On Faith and Works," can be cited which touches on the catechumenate formation during these centuries:

> "What is it that happens during the time when the catechumens keep their place and their name? They are taught what the faith and conduct of a Christian should be."[7]

But in this text Augustine says nothing about the rites celebrated during the period of the catechumenate. Undoubtedly, this is because there were none. We know that during this period, the catechumens received their formation uniquely through the Sunday celebration of the Liturgy of the Word, and that many of them did not even participate in that! The catechumenate, at one time the instrument *par excellence* of Christian formation, henceforth existed only in theory, and not in practice.[8]

Fortunately, the new Rite of 1972 highlights the value of the period of catechumenal formation and its accompanying rites. And it does so in keeping with the spirit and the rigor of the third century, the golden age of the catechumenate.

The Spirit of the Catechumenate: Patristic Images

THE Fathers of the Church used a number of images to describe one or another aspect of catechumenal pedagogy, which can also help to clarify what the early Church considered Christian initiation to be. In this section we will examine three of these images.

Military Training: Tertullian, Cyprian, and Commodian were fond of describing the catechumenate as comparable to the training which a young soldier must undergo. This image of the catechumenate was a very popular one in Northern Africa in the third century.

To understand this image, we must realize that when a young man at that time decided to enter the military, he was not given the title of "soldier" ("miles") immediately after giving up his status as "civilian." The young recruit was termed a *tiro,* or a novice. And a certain period of apprenticeship was necessary in order for him to learn how to use his arms and equipment. It was only after he proved his proficiency with his weapons that he was permitted to take the oath by which he would commit himself, at the cost of his life if necessary, to the service of his superior. When the recruit took this oath, he was marked by a tattoo indicating the leader or superior to whom he belonged.

While such a militaristic image may not seem altogether appropriate for the Church in the twentieth

century, we should be able to appreciate its importance for the Church in the third. Following St. Paul,
who compares the Christian to a soldier or an athlete,
the African Fathers (especially Cyprian)[9] stressed that
by Baptism one becomes a "soldier of Christ." Moreover, his entire life then becomes a battle with Satan,
a battle he must engage in with courage and perseverance, and, if necessary, to the point of martyrdom.
This struggle must also be carried out in a spirit of
confidence and joy, for the Christian who remains
faithful to his baptismal oath is assured of the crown
of eternal victory in heaven.

It was an easy matter, then, for the third century
Church to apply this image of military training to the
period of the catechumenate. Just as a young man
resigned his civilian status in order to become a
"novice" and begin instruction in the materials of war,
so does a convert renounce his pagan life in order to
become a catechumen and receive instruction in
matters of faith and Christian life.[10] When he has
been sufficiently prepared, the catechumen will be
admitted to baptism. At that moment, he will make his
profession of faith, an oath by which he commits
himself to Christ. Only then is he marked with the seal
of Christ.

Of all the aspects and facets of the catechumenate,
this military image seems to emphasize that (1) baptism is a commitment to live in total service to the
Lord, and (2) that this commitment presupposes a time
of apprenticeship. Without such a period of apprenticeship, no real commitment could even be made, let
alone put into practice.

The Exodus: The Fathers of the Church often compared the Christian life to the journey of the Hebrews

through the desert, a pilgrimage leading from baptism (the Christians "crossing through the Red Sea") to heaven (the promised land).[11] But Origen applies the same Exodus image to the period of the catechumenate proper.[12]

Origen parallels the Exodus journey with the steps of the catechumenal journey as follows: Egypt is the image of paganism from which the candidate must be liberated, the darkness of error and idolatry from which he must be converted, the "earthly life" which he must renounce in order to "come to a knowledge of divine law."

The crossing of the Red Sea is comparable to entrance into the catechumenate, by which he is "incorporated into the group of catechumens."

The journey in the desert represents the beginning of the spiritual life, for it is during this period of the catechumenate that the candidate "learns to obey the commandments of the Church." As Origen says, "Each day they listen to God's law and contemplate the face of Moses who reveals to us the glory of the Lord." "Amid this silence and calm, they devote themselves to the law and are impregnated with the divine word."

For Origen, the crossing of the River Jordan is analogous to the Christian's baptism, which takes place in the presence of all the clergy. Baptism "initiates into these sublime and sacred mysteries only those who have a right to approach them."

What is the promised land? For Origen it is the Christian life lived according to the precepts of the Gospel — a journey with Jesus, who "takes us by the hand and becomes the guide for our new faith."

The value of this image of the Exodus applied to the

catechumenate is that it highlights how this period is not a time for cognitive learning about the Christian life, but rather a lived experience of that life. It is a time for *listening to the Word* of God which both forms and directs the candidate. It is a style of life where one is impregnated by the Word and tries to live according to it.

The image of the Exodus also underlines the communal aspect of the catechumenal experience, involving the candidate not only with other catechumens, but with all the Christian community as well.

This image also stresses the "journey" aspect of this period of formation, a theme which appears repeatedly in the Church's earliest writings on Christian life.[13]

Gestation and Birth: The most popular image used by the early Church for the period of catechumenal formation was the image of an infant's gestation and birth, strongly influenced, no doubt, by the early Church's self-image as "mother" or "spouse."[14]

The birth of a child is not simply a one-day affair. There is first the moment of conception when the sperm of the man is received by the womb of the woman. The seed of new life thus conceived will remain for nine months in the womb to be nourished by the mother and to grow. This is the period of gestation. If the birth takes place too early in the gestation period, the infant will not survive. In this case the infant's "birth" would really be an "abortion."

Finally there comes the actual birth when the infant enters the world, but during the first few months he will need the special care necessary to keep him alive and growing.

The application of this image to the catechumenate

is readily evident.[15] Entrance into the catechumenate corresponds to the infant's conception; through the power of the Word of God, the Church has conceived a new Christian within her womb. During the time of the catechumenate, the Church nourishes these catechumens by instruction and by liturgical actions. Thus, the new Christian grows and prepares gradually to come into the world. Baptism is the birth of a member of the faithful, who, born into the very life of God, will be able to grow in and live that life to the full.

The value of this image for Christian initiation is that it demonstrates that the catechumenate period is not just a *school*. Rather, it is a living experience of growth, which takes place in the womb of the Christian community. It must be, then, a nourishing and protective environment for the candidates.

Taking these three images together we notice that in spite of their unique peculiarities there are some aspects common to all of them:

— Catechumenal initiation, like all of Christian life itself, is progressive and continuous growth.

— This growth demands a certain amount of time. The length of this time cannot be fixed in advance, but depends on the candidate's manifestation to the community of the results of his growth, experience in Christian living, and learning.

— This growth takes place between the stages of entrance into the chatechumenate and admission to the sacraments of initiation. These two stages can best be thought of as thresholds which cannot be crossed until the candidate has demonstrated to the community that he has satisfied the demanding conditions for entrance and admission.

Non-patristic Images

BESIDES these three images which the Fathers of the Church applied to the catechumenate, we might make mention of three other images. Although these images were not used explicitly by the Fathers in referring to the catechumenate, they may be helpful for us.

The Vine or Tree: The biblical image of the vine or tree stresses that the Christian life must bear abundant fruit. The planting of the seed in the ground can represent the significance of entrance into the catechumenate. The period of the catechumenate corresponds to the years of maturation and growth necessary before the plant can yield its fruits. Baptism corresponds to the point where the mature plant can now give forth its fruit.[16]

The Image of Betrothal: The image of betrothal (inspired by the biblical theme of the Covenant) stresses that the Christian life is a love relationship. Baptism is the making of a covenant, a marriage between God and the Christian. Numerous patristic commentaries on the Song of Songs speak of the Christian life as a journey of love. In keeping with this image, entrance into the catechumenate could be considered a type of betrothal, and this period of betrothal as a loving discovery of the One who is loved and lover.

The Apostolic Image: The image of the Apostles highlights the catechumenate, as well as the Christian life in general, as a life lived with Christ. It was only after they had encountered Jesus (John 1:35-51) that

Christ called them as his Apostles "to be with him" (Mark 3:13-14). This was their "entrance into the catechumenate," after they had *discovered* Jesus in his pre-catechesis.

After their call, they lived with Jesus for two or three years, listening to him, entering into discussion with him, following him, striving to follow his example. This is precisely what catechumenal formation is all about (cf. John 15:14-16). They became friends with Christ; they received his Word; they became ready to bear fruit.

Finally, they experience with Christ the paschal mystery, and then experience his invisible presence after the resurrection through the Spirit. And this parallels the experience of the newly baptized in the period of postbaptismal (mystagogical) catechesis.[17]

The Significance of the Period of Catechumenal Formation

THE RCIA, in keeping with the affirmations of the Second Vatican Council, stresses the value and significance of the catechumenal period.

Vatican II

To understand the significance of the catechumenal period in the *RCIA*, we must first examine some of the pertinent pronouncements on this subject by the Second Vatican Council. Paragraph 14 of the *Decree on the Missionary Activity of the Church* presents some essential aspects of the catechumenal period:

> The catechumenate is not a mere expounding of doctrines and precepts, but a *training period* for the whole Christian life. It is an *apprenticeship* of appropriate length, during which disciples are joined to Christ, their Teacher. Therefore, catechumens should be properly instructed in the mystery of salvation and in the practice of gospel morality. By sacred rites which are to be held at successive intervals, they should be introduced into the life of faith, liturgy, and love, which God's People live.[18]

> But this Christian initiation through the catechumenate should be taken care of not only by catechists or priests, but by the entire

community of the faithful, especially by the sponsors. Thus, right from the outset the catechumens will feel that they belong to the People of God. Since the life of the Church is an apostolic one, the catechumens should also learn to cooperate actively, by the witness of their lives and by the profession of their faith, in the spread of the Gospel and in the upbuilding of the Church.[19]

In speaking of the initial conversion in the immediately preceding paragraph (13), the Council described the catechumenate in different terms:

"By the workings of divine grace, the new convert sets out on a *spiritual journey*. Already sharing through faith in the mystery of Christ's death and resurrection, he journeys from the old man to the new one, perfected in Christ.

This *transition*, which brings with it a *progressive change* of outlook and morals, should manifest itself through its social effects, and should be gradually developed during the time of the catechumenate."[20]

Note that these two paragraphs reflect two complementary models for the catechumenate. Paragraph 14 uses the terms "training period," "apprenticeship," and "initiation." These terms depict an important aspect of the catechumenate: it is lived experience. Paragraph 13 speaks of the catechumenate in terms of "journey," "transition," and "change," stressing the aspect of ongoing education. It is these aspects of lived experience and ongoing education which the RCIA expresses and clarifies in the introductory guidelines. These guidelines enunciate the pedagogical principles underlying catechumenal initiation.

Underlying Pedagogical Principles

The RCIA specifies two pedagogical principles inherent to catechumenal initiation (18-20, 98-99).

First of all, the period of the catechumenate must afford the candidates enough time so that their faith may mature. It is a period of "pastoral formation," which "continues until they have matured sufficiently in their conversion or faith. If necessary, it may last for several years" (*RCIA*, 98). The decree stresses again that the catechumenate is "an *extended* period during which the candidates are given pastoral formation and are trained by suitable discipline," and thus "brought to maturity" (*RCIA*, 19).

The second pedagogical principle concerns the essential means by which this pastoral formation is attained: "They are nourished by the Church on the Word of God, and helped by liturgical celebrations" (*RCIA*, 18). The next paragraph develops these two means into four complementary aspects by which the faith of the catechumens is brought to maturity:

1. Catechesis, which leads the catechumens "to an intimate understanding of the mystery of salvation."
2. Experience of the Christian way of life, including prayer, witness to the faith, expectation of Christ, obedience to the Spirit, and love of neighbor.
3. Liturgical rites which purify the candidates and strengthen them with God's blessing.

4. Participation in the apostolic life of the Church by the witness of their own lives and the profession of their faith.

The Proposed Rites

THE growth in faith of the catechumens is sustained by three kinds of liturgical rites:

1. Celebrations of the Word, either by participation in the Liturgy of the Word at Mass or by other special celebrations of the Word;
2. Blessings and minor exorcisms;
3. Rites between the stages of the catechumenate.

Of course, all the members of the community involved with the initiation of the catechumens should participate in these celebrations (*RCIA*, 105). Let us now examine each of them.

Celebrations of the Word

The purpose of these celebrations is fourfold:

— to plant more deeply within the hearts of the catechumens the teaching they have received;
— to teach them different ways and aspects of prayer;
— to help them understand the signs, actions, and seasons of the liturgies;
— to enable them to enter gradually into the worship of the entire community (*RCIA*, 106).

The RCIA says nothing about the structure of celebrations of the Word apart from the Mass. But it is clear that if they are to realize the above-mentioned goals, then they must respect the principles which govern all liturgical celebration. This also goes for the minor exorcisms and blessings which will be discussed below (RCIA, 108).

As to the time for these celebrations, the new Rite simply makes two suggestions. They may be celebrated after one of the catechetical sessions (RCIA, 108). If they take place regularly on Sundays, the catechumens should participate in them faithfully and take an active part (RCIA, 107,a).

If these celebrations of the Word are conducted as the first part of the Eucharist, then they can be helpful for gradually introducing the candidates into the worship of the community. If possible the dismissal of the catechumens should take place after the liturgy of the Word, and a petition for them is added in the general intercessions. Care should be taken that the candidates are dismissed in a friendly manner and that this does not cause difficulty or misunderstanding.[21]

The Minor Exorcisms and the Blessings

The minor exorcisms of the catechumenate period differ from the major exorcisms of the Lenten period. The Lenten exorcisms are imperative in form, ordering Satan to depart. The minor exorcisms, however, are deprecative, that is, constructed in the form of a prayer asking for God's help in the struggle to live out the Christian life. They are to "show the catechumens the true nature of the spiritual life as a battle between flesh and spirit, and underlines both the importance of self denial in order to gain the blessings of the Kingdom of God and the continuing need of God's help" (RCIA, 101). The Rite gives six models for the minor exorcisms in paragraphs 113-118 and five more in the appendix (*RCIA*, 373).

The exorisms are normally conducted by the priest or deacon, but the bishop can delegate a suitable catechist for this function. The catechumens bow their heads or kneel down, and the minister prays over them while extending his hands over their heads. The exorcisms may be celebrated during a liturgy of the Word, at the beginning or end of one of the regular meetings of the catechumens. For special reasons, the exorcism may be celebrated privately for an individual candidate.[22]

The blessings are prayers to bring the catechumens the courage, joy, and peace they need to continue their efforts and journey.[23] They are a visible expression to the catechumens of God's love and the Church's care for them. As models for these blessings, paragraphs 121-124 give four examples, and the appendix lists five more (*RCIA*, 374).

The blessings need not be performed by a priest or deacon, but can be celebrated by a catechist, who needs no special delegation by the bishop to do this. In saying the prayer of blessing, the minister extends his hands over the catechumens. Then, if possible, the catechumens approach the celebrant, who lays hands on each one. The blessing may be given at the end of a liturgy of the Word, at the end of a catechetical session, or when it may be particularly beneficial for the catechumen to experience this sign of God's love and the Church's concern.

The Rites Between the Stages of the Catechumenate

The new Rite (103) mentions that it may be beneficial to mark the passage of the catechumen from one catechetical group or level by an appropriate rite of transition. The RCIA gives a selection of such rites, with the reminder that they should not be celebrated unless and until the catechumens give evidence of a maturation in faith (*RCIA*, 125).

The RCIA leaves latitude for a number of possibilities in celebrating these rites.

The "rites of passage" may simply be the anticipation of some of the rites normally associated with the Lenten period of purification and enlightenment (*RCIA*, 126). Since the Lenten period is so short, and consequently there may not be an opportunity to celebrate them at that time, it might be well to celebrate them as rites of transition within the period of the catechumenate. These anticipated rites would include the presentation of the Creed, or the Our Father, followed by the rite of Ephpheta (opening of the ears and mouth); or the profession of the Creed, in which case the rite of Ephpheta should precede it.

Another possibility would be to mark the passage through the different levels of the catechumenate by an anointing with the oil of catechumens (*RCIA*, 127), which could be repeated.[24] The anointing can be done by either a priest or a deacon. The essential components of this rite include (1) a minor exorcism, accompanied by the formula in RCIA 130; and (2) an anointing on the breast, or on both hands, or even on other parts of the body if it would be appropriate. The oil used is the Oil of Catechumens, blessed by the bishop at the Chrism Mass. For pastoral reasons, the oil may be blessed by the priest himself in the course of the celebration.

Pastoral Suggestions

CONCERNING the rites which mark the progress of the candidates through the period of the catechumenate, the new Rite throws the doors wide open to liturgical creativity. Unfortunately, little has been done with regard to the rites of the catechumenate, most of the liturgical efforts having been directed toward the major rites of entrance into the catechumenate and the rites of the Lenten period. What follows are some reflections on the attempts and experiments to create and implement the rites of the catechumenal period which can guide our own efforts.

Rites Between the Stages of the Catechumenate

Among the many innovations of the new Rite, the rites celebrated between the stages of the catechumenate are among the most interesting from a pastoral point of view.

When the catechumenate (in the strict sense) extends over a two- or a three-year period,[25] it would be abnormal if there were no liturgical rites to sustain the catechumens on their journey. When they pass from the first year class to the second, or from the second to the third, it would be appropriate to mark this transition by an appropriate rite. These rites would then break up the long catechumenate by clearly recognized stages, leading to Baptism—similar to the way stations or road-side restaurants which mark one's progress relative to the final destination on a trip along a highway.

Anointing the catechumens seems to be emerging as the preferred format for these rites of transition. It also seems to be the most appropriate in view of the symbolism of the anointing: the power and strength which God gives the catechumens to sustain them in their conversion. Vatican II calls this conversion a progressive passage from the old man to the new, and "since the Lord he believes in is a sign of contradiction, the convert often experiences human breaks and separations. But he also tastes the joy which God gives without measure."[26] The help which God gives is constant throughout the entire catechumenal journey, and not given in two installments—at the very beginning (entrance into the catechumenate) and the very end (enrollment of names). Thus, in some African dioceses a rite of anointing marks the passage from the first to the second year of catechesis. Other dioceses defer this anointing to mark the passage from the second year to the third.

Another, and less frequently used, format for conducting rites of transition is to anticipate the celebration of the Presentations (RCIA, 181-193). In some locales, where there is a two-year catechumenate period, the Creed is presented at the end of the first year. We personally feel, however, that it would be better to present the Our Father at the end of the first year, and to defer the presentation of the Creed to the end of the second year (if there is a three-year catechumenate) or during the Lenten period (if the catechumenate period lasts two years).

If an anointing is preferred over an anticipation of the Presentations, the following schema developed by and used in an African diocese for the past ten years may be of interest:

Liturgy of the Word: The texts used emphasize the necessity of an authentic Christian life, the importance of perseverance, and the values of fidelity. Such texts include:

— Isaiah 1:16-20 or 2 Mac. 6:18-31
— Ephesians 6:10-17 or Rev. 3:1-6
— Matt. 4:1-11; Mk 4:10-20; Lk 11:21-28; John 12:25-26, 31-32; John 17:11-26.

A meditation song and the homily should highlight the important human attitudes suggested by these texts.

The Anointing: First comes the exorcism and blessing of the oil, with a more developed prayer than the one suggested in *RCIA,* 131.[27] A dialogue between the priest and the catechumens then follows, which highlights their willingness to persevere in the efforts toward full conversion and preparation for Baptism. This is followed by the anointing, in which the priest presents the oil and says the formula given in *RCIA,* 130. The sponsors then anoint the catechumens on the breast, the shoulders, and the arms.

Prayer: The ceremony concludes with a minor exorcism and imposition of hands by the celebrant, general intercessions for the catechumens, a final blessing, and dismissal.

Note that among the communities which use anointing as a rite of transition, some repeat it towards the end of the Lenten period of enlightenment (*RCIA,* 206-207) and others do not.

Celebration of the Word

Because of the wide variety among the different celebrations of the Word developed by communities for use within the period of the catechumenate, we can only present here some of the more noteworthy attempts.

Special celebrations of the Word (that is, distinct from the Liturgy of the Word at a Eucharistic celebration) for catechumens are becoming more frequent. They should have the following characteristics:

> First, they must be *genuine celebrations,* and not catechetical lessons. The assembly of believers joyfully celebrate one or another aspect of the Christian mystery perceived as real and lived by the community as a saving event. It's a question of *celebration* rather than discussion, of *experience* rather than explanation, of *living* rather than learning. Such a liturgy is more effective if celebrated *before* the catechesis rather than after. Liturgy is not just another activity within catechesis; it is the very source of catechesis.[28] In order to be educative, these special celebrations must respect the fundamental principles inherent to all liturgical action.
>
> Secondly, these celebrations must promote to the maximum the participation, expression, and comprehension of the catechumens. Special celebrations, moreso than Liturgies of the Word within the context of Eucharistic celebrations, furnish the community with a great possibility for creativity, keeping in mind, however, the general liturgical principles which must govern all creative experiments:
>
> *Liturgy is participation.* Opportunities for participation include not just the readings,

the songs, and the prayers, but also gestures, which can involve the community, and silence—at times of meditation and adoration.

Liturgy is living expression. It is incarnated in the means of expression proper to the local culture. Consequently liturgy must respect these means of expression if the catechumens are to discover within it an agent of the Christian mystery lived concretely by the community.

Liturgy is profound understanding. This level of comprehension is not reached by process of logical reasoning, but only by discovering symbolic activity as much more convincing than rational discourse.

While the participation of the catechumens in the first part of the Mass is to be encouraged, it nevertheless poses two kinds of problems for which there are no easy solutions.

The first problem deals with the fact that the Sunday liturgies are generally not geared to the catechumens. The choice of the readings, the homily, the prayers, and gestures are all governed by the needs and worship style of those who have already been baptized—most likely for many years. A second problem arises in deciding what to do with the catechumens after the Liturgy of the Word. Should they reassemble in a separate place (to our mind, the preferable solution), or should they remain in the church with the faithful?

Possible solutions to these two types of problems might include the following suggestions. Concerning the participation of the catechumens in the Liturgy of the Word, two approaches seem to be developing. In some areas, the Liturgy of the Word is designed and appropriate readings selected each week with the catechumens directly in mind. This solution has been successful in areas where a Christian community is just beginning to be formed. But it has also been helpful in more established communities where the members need to be re-evangelized.

On the other hand, others prefer to use the readings and prayers which the lectionary and sacramentary suggest, but adapt them to make the liturgy more understandable to the catechumens. This consists in retaining two or only one of the readings for the day, and in leaving more time to explain, meditate on, and assimilate the proclaimed Word.

Concerning the second part of the Mass, the dismissal of the catechumens just before it begins is rarely done. And this is unfortunate. In places where it is done, the catechumens reassemble immediately with their chatechists and certain sponsors to deepen their faith in the celebrated Word.

Most often, the catechumens remain in church with the larger community until the end of the Mass. But the danger here is that the catechumens can become too used to "assisting" at a liturgical action whose full significance can be appreciated only to the extent that all participate. The danger is not just for the catechumens, but for the faithful as well who often are content to "assist" rather than actively *participate*.

The Minor Exorcisms and Blessings

Instead of being celebrated in their own right, the minor exorcisms and blessings are usually tacked on to other rites and celebrations. This fact reveals that the unique value of the minor exorcisms and blessings is not yet sufficiently recognized. Moreover the formulas for these rites as proposed in the RCIA need to be reworked, and adapted more to the language and customs of the local culture. Only then, perhaps, will they gain their full significance. As with so many aspects of the new Rite, and in particular all the rites of the catechumenate period, creative liturgical experimentation and adaptation remains a most pressing and immediate concern.

Notes

[1] The catechumens were also separated from the faithful in the agapé meals (*AT* 27). They are present for the meal, but they receive only a "bread of exorcism" (*AT* 26, 28). No serious study has been done on just what this "bread of exorcism" was.

[2] Cf. Michel Dujarier, *Le Parrainage des adultes aux trois premiers siècles de l'Eglise; recherche historique sur l'évolution des garanties et des étapes catéchuménales avant 313*, Paris: Editions du Cerf, 1962. Hippolytus' description is also confirmed in Syrian documents dating from the third century, especially the *Didascalia Apostolorum*. Cf. *Didascalia Apostolorum* (Syriac version), translated and accompanied by the Verona Latin fragments, with an introduction and notes by R. Hugh Connolly, Oxford: Clarendon Press, 1929.

[3] Pierre Nautin, *Origène: sa vie et son oeuvre*, Paris: Beauchesne, 1977, especially "Les Homélies," pp. 389-409. Cf. also Pierre Nautin, *Origène: Homélies sur Jérémie*, tome I in the series Sources chrétiennes, n. 232 (1976), especially "L'assemblée quotidienne," pp. 111-112.

[4] At the time of Hippolytus, it appears that a morning liturgy of the Word was not always held every day. In principle, the community gathered daily for a liturgy of the Word (*AT* 39), but in fact, on some days this assembly did not take place (*AT* 41).

[5] Clement of Alexandria, *Paidagogus (Christ the Educator)*, II, 96, 2. Cf. also, *AT* 35.

[6] Pierre Nautin, *Origène: Homélies sur Jérémie, op. cit., pp. 105-112.*

[7] Augustine, *De fide et operibus*, VI, 9.

[8] R. De Latte, "St. Augustin et le baptême. Etude liturgico-historique du rituel baptismal des adultes chez saint Augustin," in *Questions liturgiques*, 1976, pp. 117-223, in particular, pp. 189-191.

[9] José Company, *"Miles Christi" en la espiritualidad de San Cipriano*, Barcelona, 1956.

[10] For more information on the technical names applied to the catechumenate, see Tertullian, *De paenitentia*, VI and 14; and Commodianus, *Instructiones*, II, 5.

[11] C. Spicq, *Vie chrétienne et pérignination selon le Nouveau Testament*, Paris: Editions du Cerf, 1972 (Lection Divina #72).

[12] Origen, *Homily on Numbers*, XXVI, 4; and *Homilia in Jesu Nave*, IV, 1.

[13] For the Christian life as a "race," cf. Phil. 3; as a "pilgrimage,"

Hebrews; as "ascension," the writings of the Fathers.

[14]Karl Delahaye, *"Ecclesia Mater" chez les Pères de l'Eglise,* Paris: Editions du Cerf, 1964 (Unam Sanctam).

[15]For a more complete treatment of this image for the catechumenate, see Michel Dujarier, "Le catéchuménat et la maternité de l'Eglise," in *Maison Dieu,* 71, pp. 78-93.

[16]For the image of the vine (John 15:1-8) and the tree (Luke 13:6-9) see Clement of Alexandria, *Stromata (The Miscellanies),* II, 95, 3 – 96, 2; and Cyril of Jerusalem, *Procatechesis,* 11.

[17]This image of the catechumenate, drawn from the formation of the Apostles by Christ, does not appear to have been used by the Fathers of the Church.

[18]"Decree on the Missionary Activity of the Church," par. 14, in *The Documents of Vatican II,* edited by Walter M. Abbot, S.J., London: Geoffrey Chapman, 1967, pp. 600-601.

[19]*Ibid.,* p. 601.

[20]*Ibid.,* par. 13, p. 600.

[21]Cf. RCIA 107b, and 19, 3. Also André Laurentin and Michel Dujarier, *Catéchuménat: données de l'histoire et perspectives nouvelles,* Paris: Editions du Centurion, 1969.

[22]It is difficult to understand why the new Rite recommends the celebrations of the exorcisms "before the catechumenate, during the time of evangelization . . . for the spiritual good of interested inquirers" (*RCIA,* 111). Should not these sacramentals be reserved for "christians"—those converts who have already been liturgically admitted to the Church through entrance into the catechumenate? The same is true for the blessings (*RCIA,* 120).

[23]It is surprising that in regard to the catechumenal blessings, the new Rite says that the candidates "still lack the grace of the sacraments" (*RCIA,* 102). Of course, they are not yet baptized. But we should not forget that their initiation has already begun, since by the rite of entrance into the catechumenate they have already received a "first consecration" (*RCIA,* 14), and if they have the proper disposition, the Holy Spirit already dwells within them. On this point, see Origen's *Homily on Numbers,* III, 1.

[24]The Rite also indicates that "for special reasons, it may also be given privately for individuals" (*RCIA,* 128).

[25]To be more precise, we should perhaps say one and a half years, or two and a half years, since the catechetical year generally begins in the Fall, with Baptism celebrated normally in the Spring, at the Easter Vigil.

[26]"Decree on the Missionary Activity of the Church," *op. cit.,* par. 13, p. 600.

[27]For examples of more developed prayers, the reader can draw from *Trois antiques rituels du baptême,* by A. Salles, Paris: Editions du Cerf,

1958, *Sources chrétiennes* series.

[28]The reader would do well to draw the pastoral consequences from the excellent work of J. Dournes, *L'offrande des peuples*, Paris: Editions du Cerf, 1967, Chapters 23 and 24.

Chapter 3
The Rite of Election

IN the previous chapter we showed how the journey of Christian initiation is made up of two periods, each leading to an important threshold or stage. There is a period of pre-evangelization which culminates with entry into the catechumenate—the first stage. With this ceremony, the Church recognizes the convert as "Christian," and draws him into her womb for an extended period of growth and formation.

The second period is one of education in faith and evangelical life. This is the period of the "catechumen-ate" properly speaking, during which the community brings the new Christian to a discovery of the teaching of Christ and instructs him in how to live a truly Christian life. This second period leads to the second threshold: the state of election. By this ceremony of election, the Church calls the catechumen to the reception of the sacraments of initiation, which will make him a member of the faithful. It is this second stage, celebrated at the beginning of Lent, to which we now turn our attention.

Historical Overview

Two very different periods at the beginning of the Church's history had a marked influence on the development of the rite of election. The first, during the second and third centuries, was the period of persecution during which the catechumenate was born. The second, covering the fourth and fifth centuries, saw the catechumenate develop in a milieu not only freed from persecution but which had become more or less totally Christianized.

Second and Third Centuries

In its earliest origins, the catechumenate was distinguished by a rather lengthy liturgical preparation for Baptism, which set rigorous and stringent criteria for those who wished to become Christian. During this epoch, Baptism itself was a celebration spread out over the course of several days, within a context of community prayer. This format is confirmed by a number of early documents.

Already at the end of the first century, the *Didache* gives evidence of the role of the communal prayer in the baptismal celebration:

> Before the Baptism, may the one baptizing, along with those already baptized, and others who are able, observe, first, a fast. To the baptized, you should impose a preliminary fast of one or two days.[1]

Around 150, St. Justin reveals that during these days of liturgical preparation catechumens are taught "to pray and beseech God, in fasting, to forgive all their past sins, while we pray and fast with them." [2]

The same practice is found in the pseudo-Clementine writings. [3] According to the testimony of Hippolytus and Tertullian, this preparation seems to have lasted for one week, accompanied by repeated exorcisms.

Given our immediate concern with the rite of election, we must note and emphasize that *no one* could be admitted to this week of preparatory celebration for Baptism without having been called by God, and without having been chosen by the Church. This choice certainly presupposes certain conditions which we will now examine.

St. Justin urges his candidates, not only to, "believe as true the things we teach and say," but also, "to give assurance that they will be able to live them."[4] Thus, it is not just the faith of the candidates which was scrutinized, but also their behavior, because Christian faith is authentic only to the extent that it transforms the life of the believer.

This is what Origen will say one hundred years later when he will insist on admitting only those "who have demonstrated as best they can their resolve to do only what is fitting for Christians."[5]

This rigorous approach is still more evident in the *Apostolic Tradition* of Hippolytus of Rome.

> When selecting those who are to be baptized, the life of the candidates is to be closely examined: Have they lived honestly while they were catechumens? Have they honored the widows? Have they visitied the sick? Have

they done all sorts of good works? If those
who lead them to the Church testify for each
one, saying that they acted thus, then they
will hear the Gospel.[6]

In North Africa, Tertullian vigorously affirms the
same view:

The Lord will first verify the quality of the
repentance (i.e., of the effective conversion
of the catechumen) before according to us so
magnificent a reward as eternal life (in Baptism) . . . This bath of Baptism is the seal
of faith; but this faith is based on and in
turn is complemented by the sincerity of
repentance.[7]

The state of affairs in the earliest days of the
catechumenate is thus very clear. Only those whose
lives had been transformed by faith were admitted to
the reception of Baptism.

After this examination of their lives and behavior,
"those who had been set apart" are called "the elect,"
that is "the chosen ones"—chosen by God, for
through the Church, it is God who has "elected"
them, and his choosing is an utterly gratuitous gift of
divine love.

Fourth and Fifth Centuries

From the fourth century onwards, when the Roman
state recognized Christianity as legitimate, and the
Church was at last protected—even privileged—by the
government, conversions were not always as serious
as they had to be in the previous period of persecution. Many of the Christians entered the catechumen-

ate for rather self-interested motives and without real conviction of faith. They were Christians in name only and did not bother to follow the instructions as they should have. To remedy this grossly insufficient preparation, the Church developed the week of baptismal celebration. This eventually was lengthened to cover the seven weeks of Lent, which thus became a time of intensive formation.

But the preparation for this Lenten formation period began with Christmas and Epiphany, at which time the bishop preached on the necessity of Baptism and invited those catechumens who were still hesitating to come "give their name" as the sign of their readiness for immediate preparation for the sacraments of initiation at the next Easter celebration.

There was thus instituted in the fourth century a ceremony taking place at the beginning of Lent, which corresponded to the more ancient ceremony, attested to by Hippolytus of Rome, of choosing the candidates for Baptism eight days before Easter. This new ceremony was called the "enrollment of names."

We possess an excellent description of this ceremony in writings of Egeria, a Spaniard, who recorded her observations of such a ceremony during her pilgrimage to Jerusalem near the end of the fourth century:

> The one who gives his name does so on the day before the beginning of Lent, and a priest notes all the names . . . The next day, the beginning of Lent, the day on which the eight weeks begin, the candidates are led forward one by one. If they are men, they come with their godfather; if they are women, with their godmother. Then the Bishop questions the neighbors of each of the candidates, saying,

97

"Does he lead an honest life?" "Does he respect his parents?" "Does he refrain from drunkenness and lying?", covering all the more serious human failings. If the candidate is recognized as without reproach by all those interrogated in the presence of witnesses, the Bishop writes his name in his own hand. But if he is accused on some point, the Bishop has him leave, saying "May he reform, and when he has reformed, he will proceed towards Baptism."[8]

This text reveals well the care taken to verify the quality of life of the candidates, and the intervention not only of the godparents but also of the "neighbors" who must testify on their behalf. Unfortunately, the catechumens who presented themselves at the beginning of Lent were sometimes far from sufficiently prepared, as is evident from the *Procatechesis* of Cyril.

The same kind of ceremony that Egeria describes was most likely practiced outside of Jerusalem as well. Theodore of Mopsuestia describes such a ceremony of enrollment in Antioch:

> May whoever wishes to proceed to the gift of Holy Baptism present himself to the Church of God. He will be received by one delegated to do so, according to the established custom for inscribing those progressing toward Baptism, who will take stock of the candidate's life. This office is filled, for those who are baptized, by one who is called the " guarantor."[9]

However, this ceremony took place rather late, perhaps only two weeks before Easter, due to the lack of preparation of the candidates—a situation emphasized in the writings of St. John Chrysostom.

From the moment of this state of admission to immediate preparation for Baptism, the catechumens were then called "the elect" (elected by God), or the *illuminandi* (those who are in the process of being enlightened). Later, they were called the *competentes*—those who strive together for Baptism. Unfortunately, this last name is less expressive of the reality it designates, since it emphasizes more the advancement and effort of those interested in Baptism, rather than the gratuitousness of the call and gift of God.

Even after the disappearance of the catechumenate, this rite was still maintained in the Baptismal ritual, but it became devoid of real meaning since it no longer corresponded to a real journey of lived faith.

Today we celebrate this state of admission to Baptism under the title of "Rite of Election" or the "Enrollment of Names," or better yet, and to avoid giving the impression that it is a question of election by people, "The Decisive Call."

Having treated the historical elements of this rite, we now direct our attention to its significance.

The Meaning of the Rite of Election

In what sense does the RCIA designate the rite of election as "the turning point in the whole catechumenate" (*RCIA*, 23)?

As in all the stages, we have to consider conjointly the action of God realized by the Church, and the personal advancement of the catechumens.

The action of God, realized by the Church, is the *election*. In effect, by this rite of decisive call the Church declares that those who are "chosen by God" may proceed to the sacraments. She makes manifest those whom God calls gratuitously to his life (*RCIA*, 22). And this is why, where it is possible, it is preferred that the bishop himself, or his delegate, preside at the celebration of this stage (*RCIA*, 138).

The personal advancement of the catechumens is expressed in the inscription of names. At the conclusion of the catechumenate, which is a "lengthy formation of the mind and heart" (*RCIA*, 134), the candidates manifest "their willingness to receive the sacraments" (*RCIA*, 133) and to "follow Christ with an even greater generosity" (*RCIA*, 134).

In order to be celebrated in a genuine way, this stage of election presupposes that the Church has discerned those candidates who are properly disposed to take part in sacramental initiation (*RCIA*, 22).

Because it is the Church who calls, it is the Church who is responsible for this discernment. The bishop, the priests, the deacons, the catechists, the godparents and the whole local community, each according to his responsibility, "must weigh the matter carefully and make their decision"(*RCIA*, 135). It is necessary that "before the liturgical rite is celebrated, they must have deliberated on the suitability of the candidates" (*RCIA*, 137).

The communal aspect of this deliberation is strongly emphasized in the RCIA. It even specifies that "if circumstances permit, the assembly of the catechumens themselves may also take part" (*RCIA*, 137). But on what is this discrenment based?

On the part of the catechumens, the rite of election presupposes "an enlightened faith and a deliberate intention to receive the sacraments of the Church" (*RCIA*, 134). In concrete terms this means (1) a sufficient knowledge of Christ and his teaching which makes possible an enlightened and living faith; (2) a sufficient conversion of mind and morals, manifested in a genuine striving in uprightness, in prayer, and in charity; and (3) a clear and free intention to receive the sacraments and to assume the demands they involve for daily life, because Baptism is not the end, but the beginning of a journey (*RCIA*, 23).

It should go without saying that the participation of the entire community is important, both by their presence and by their prayer, "so that the entire Church may lead the elect with her to encounter Christ" (*RCIA*, 135), and "shine with good example and continue along the way of the paschal mystery together with the elect" (*RCIA*, 142).

In particular, the godparents should exercise their liturgical office and in doing so express their own commitment. During the liturgy, "they come forward with the catechumens, and testify in their behalf before the community, and, if desired, they write their names with them in the register" (*RCIA*, 136).

Through this liturgical action, they commit themselves to "accompany" their godchild, not only during the immediate preparation for Baptism and the time of mystagogical catechesis, but also during what follows—helping the neophyte to remain faithful to what he or she promised in Baptism. Concretely, it is the task of the godparent to "show in a friendly way the place of the Gospel in his own life and in society, to help him in doubts and anxieties, to give public testimony for him, and to watch over the progress of his baptismal life" (*RCIA*, 43). It is this mission which the celebrant explicitly confers upon the godparent in the course of the celebration of the rite of election (*RCIA*, 147).

It is the responsibility of the celebrant (the bishop or his delegate) to (1) stress, in the course of the celebration, the religious and ecclesial meaning of this state (*RCIA*, 138); (2) to lead the dialogue with the community and with the catechumens before making the decision in the name of God to admit the elect; (3) to proclaim, in the name of Christ and of the Church, the divine call and the admission of the elect; and (4) to exhort the faithful as well as the catechumens to live intensely the weeks of Lent, so that Lent becomes a community retreat to prepare for the paschal solemnities.

Normally, the rite of election takes place on the first Sunday of Lent so as to impress upon all that Lent is the period of final preparation of the elect, as "a more intense preparation of the heart, which involves spiritual recollection more than catechesis" (*RCIA*, 25). This "baptismal retreat" has two functions: on one hand, a purification of the mind and heart through examination of conscience and repentance, and on the other hand, enlightenment of the elect by a deeper knowledge of Christ the Savior.

For pastoral reasons, however, and particularly in the more remote mission areas, this rite of election may be celebrated on a day other than the first Sunday of Lent. But it should always be near the beginning of Lent, during the week which either precedes or follows the first Sunday.

The Structure of the Rite of Election

RECALL, first of all, that the rite of election marks the entrance into the baptismal retreat. It presupposes, therefore, that the discernment of the worthy candidates for the sacraments has been done before this stage, so that for the elect and the entire community, Lent may truly be a baptismal retreat, undisturbed by questions or decisions which should have already been settled.

The Liturgy of the Word

Before going into the various elements which comprise the rite of election itself, let us first reflect upon the Liturgy of the Word which precedes the Rite.

The Liturgy of the Word focuses our attention on the essential condition of *an enlightened faith* which insures that this rite will be lived out after its celebration. Since this rite is normally to be celebrated on the first Sunday of Lent (*RCIA*, 139), the scriptural texts for that day correspond very well to the meaning of this stage. The first two readings concentrate on the fundamental theme of Baptism.

- Year A: Salvation, creation, sin, and grace: Gen. 2:7-9 and 3:1-7a; Romans 5:12-19.
- Year B: The Covenant of Life: its announcement to Noah realized in Baptism: Gen. 9:8-15, 1 Pet. 3:18-22.

— Year C: The Profession of faith, first of the Israelite people, then of the Christian people: Deut. 26:4-10, Romans 10:8-13.

The Gospel for the "A" Cycle depicts the temptation of Christ which reminds us of the three demands of faithfulness to the Word of God (Mt.4:4), faithfulness to the will of God (Mt.4:7), and faithfulness to the worship of God (Mt.4:10). (Full text: Mt. 4:1-11.)

If the rite is celebrated on a day other than the first Sunday of Lent, the readings from that Sunday may still be used, or other suitable readings may be chosen (RCIA, 141), highlighting such themes as:

1. *Theme of inscription of the names*
— Exodus 33:12-17: God knows us by name and journeys with us.
— Rev. 21:9b-12a, 22-27: The Lord is the New Jerusalem, accessible only to those who are purified and whose name is inscribed in the book of life.
— Luke 10:1-11, 17-20: The mission of the seventy-two disciples whose names are written in heaven.

2. *Theme of faithfulness of our response to the gratuitious call of God*
— Deut. 4:32-40: There is only one God, who has chosen us by his love, and to whom we must be faithful.
— Deut. 8:1-7: God has freed us and promises us a land of blessings if we are faithful to him.
— Ephes. 4:17-24: Live in Christ a new style of life.
— John 15:8-17: It is Jesus who has chosen us

out of love; it is for us to love him faithfully and to bear fruit.

The Rite Itself

The rite is celebrated after the homily, and comprises four parts:

1. *The Presentation of the Candidate to the Celebrant (RCIA, 143)*. This is not simply a formality, but the expression of all the educational endeavors realized by the community during the period of the catechumenate. It is also an invitation for those eager to receive the sacraments to enter more deeply into the life of the community, as well as an invitation for the community to enter into more total communion with the candidate.

   The presentation of the candidates is made either by the priest in charge of the catechumenate, by the deacons, by the catechists, or by the delegate of the community. The formula indicated in *RCIA*, 143 is only a suggestion. It would be better if the one presenting the candidates for election could do so in his or her own words.

   The celebrant then asks those who are to be elected to come forward. The candidates are then called by name, one after the other, and they take their places, along with their godparents, before the celebrant.

2. *The Deliberation of the Community*. The deliberation is led by the celebrant, who speaks to the sponsors, the community, and the candidates themselves *(RCIA, 144-146)*.

   From the godparents, he asks for their testimony on the three key elements of faith, life, and community:

the faithfulness of their godchildren in listening to the world of God proclaimed by the Church; their efforts to live out the words they have heard; and their participation in the life of charity and in prayer with the community.

To the congregation ("if desired"), the celebrant asks if they agree with what the sponsors have said (*RCIA*, 144b).

To the catechumens, the celebrant explains that the Church of Christ calls them to the sacraments of initiation. He then asks them if they are willing to answer that call.

3. *The Election Itself.* The election is expressed both by the candidates and by the Church. The catechumens respond to God's call by giving their names, either (1) by writing their names in the register; (2) by speaking their names to their sponsors who in turn inscribe them in the register; or (3) a list of the names of all the candidates is handed to the celebrant. An appropriate song may be sung, such as Ps. 15.

The celebrant in turn expresses the choice that God has made of the elect *(RCIA,* 147) by announcing the list of names chosen to be initiated at the next Easter celebration and by entrusting them to their godparents so that they may help them by their word and example in their journey towards the sacraments. The godparents express their willingness to assume responsibility by placing their hands on the shoulders of their godchildren, or by appropriate gesture.

4. *The Prayer For the Elect.* The rite of election concludes with a litany-like prayer *(RCIA,* 148 or 375) for the elect and for all those who will help them — catechists,

godparents, families, and the community. The celebrant concludes this litany with an oration. The elect are dismissed *(RCIA,* 150), and the celebration of the Eucharist follows *(RCIA,* 151).

Points for Critical Reflection

RECALL once more that the schema proposed by the RCIA is only a guide. The formulations and gestures are given as suggestions. It remains for the Christian communities, under the responsibility of their Episcopal Conferences, to adapt the texts and rites according to local customs and mentality.

As we mentioned earlier, the Christian community plays a particularly active role in the rite of election (just as they do in the rite of entrance into the catechumenate). For it is the entire Church who calls to itself new brothers and sisters, while at the same time committing itself to support them.

Thus, we must stress the role of the celebrant (the bishop or his delegate), who acts as the father of the community. We must also be careful that the dialogue between the celebrant and the community involves all those who exercise areas of responsibility (catechists, godparents, leaders of the community) as well as with the community itself. In addition to the dialogue with and interventions of the community already noted, we could, for example, have the intentions of the prayer of the faithful voiced not by just one lector, but by the representatives of the various areas of the community's responsibility.

Having recognized the importance of the inscription of the name of the candidate during the rite of election, we should also consider the importance of the name itself. The RCIA proposes that the candidates for Baptism by given a *new* name, either (1) on

Holy Saturday evening during the rites immediately preceding Baptism (*RCIA*, 203-205), or, if it would seem easier or more logical, at the moment of Baptism; or (2) at the moment of entrance into the catechumenate (*RCIA*, 88), that is, when the convert is admitted into the Church.

But could we not also consider the giving of this new name at the moment of the Rite of Election, seeing that an important part of the rite is the inscription of names? Even if the new name was already given prior to the rite of election, it would be good to remind the participants that a new name signifies the new commitment and the new way of living called for by the rite of election.

Some Critical Reflections on the Structure of the Rite

The RCIA does not seem to stress sufficiently that the rite of election is at its heart a gratuitous call from God himself. The first "call" of the candidates (*RCIA*, 143) seems to be nothing more than a simple summons to step forward in front of the celebrant. The candidates are then asked to give a concrete sign of their response to the *call from God* (inscription of names, *RCIA*, 146) even though this "call from God" has been alluded to only in very general terms (*RCIA*, 146). It is only after the concrete sign of response to God's call has been given that this "calling forward" is alluded to as being in reality a call from God himself (*RCIA*,147), almost as if the call from God were the *consequence* of (not the condition for) the catechumenal journey. In effect, the cart has been placed before the horse. Moreover, no direct and explicit call to each individual takes place in the rite. This defect is proved by the fact that the ritual directs the celebrant to explain briefly the meaning of the rite which has just occurred, (*RCIA*, 147). If the call from God was expressed clearly enough by the rite itself, there would be no need to explain it, and certainly not of explaining it after the response.

We propose, then, that the normal order of things should be respected. The gratuitous call from God comes first. The inscription of names is simply a response to that call, and should therefore come second. We suggest, then, the following general structure for the Rite of Election:

First, a collective presentation (not calling out of individual names) of the candidates by the delegate of the catechumenate or of the community.

Secondly, the deliberation by the community, led by the celebrant. This must be developed more than it is at present in *RCIA* 145 and based on a real dialogue, and always with all those responsible for the catechumens (and not just the godparents): with the assembly (by *necessity*, and not *"if desired"* as the New Rite unfortunately specifies in *RCIA*, 144) and with the catechumens, who express at last their desire and intention (but without yet giving their names).

Thirdly, the call of the elect could be carried out in two ways: the call is determined and proclaimed, in the name of the Church, and therefore, in the name of God, by the calling of each candidate by name, done by the celebrant. The call is then ratified by the elect themselves, by means of an oral response to the calling by name, and by means of one gesture or another, such as the act of moving to a position before or next to the celebrant, and perhaps of receiving an imposition of hands, and lastly of giving or writing his or her name.

The second stage—the rite of election—seems to be in need of more critical attention and refinement than any of the other stages as delineated in the *RCIA*. It seems to many to be a bit abstract, at least as it is presented in the New Rite. But it can have, nonetheless, great pastoral value if we can determine a way or ways of expressing its meaning and of bringing it to life in a concrete way. Can we exercise the creativity necessary to give to this stage all its richness of call and commitment and its communal dimensions?

It would also be good to emphasize more the joy and the work of grace which flow from this call. The joy must spring forth spontaneously from a dialogue which is not just a juridical contract but the lived expression of a deep desire and of an intense friendship. The songs and acclamations should also express joy, not just of the elect but of the entire community.

Finally, the concluding prayer could also better manifest the work of grace. In its present form in the *RCIA*, this prayer is unfortunately reduced to a prayer of petition. When are we going to rediscover the eucharistic dimension of all prayer and even more so of all celebration?

Notes

[1] *Didache* , VII,4.
[2] Justin, *I Apol.*, 61,2.
[3] Pseudo-Clementine, *Rec.* VI,15; *Hom.* 3 ,73 and XIII,9, and 12.
[4] Justin, *I Apol.*, 61,2.
[5] Origen, *Contra Celsum (Against Celsus)*, III,51,5.
[6] *AT*, 20.
[7] Tertullian, *De paenitentia*, 6.
[8] *Pilgrimage of Egeria*, 45.
[9] Theodore of Mopsuestia, *Homily*, XII,14.

Chapter 4
The Scrutinies

THE Scrutinies have the honor of being the most misunderstood, and consequently the most mis-celebrated, of the rites of initiation. They are often relegated to the role of exorcisms, although exorcism is only one element of this rite. And most often attention is focused on the action of God in these rites, forgetting the indispensable participation of man.

If there is to be a genuine restoration of these traditional rites of the initiation process, then we must begin by studying the history and the meaning of the scrutinies.

Historical Overview of the Scrutinies

In studying the history of the scrutinies,[1] as in studying the history of any of the rites of Christian initiation, care must be taken not to base one's study solely on the liturgical works of the sixth and.seventh centuries. The catechumenate reached its high point several centuries earlier, and so in order to understand the meaning and the place of the scrutinies within the ensemble of Christian initiation, we must return to the very sources. Even though the term "scrutinies" was not used in the earliest centuries, it is to those earliest times that we must return in order to discover how the scrutinies evolved.

Second and Third Centuries

In his excellent work on the history of the liturgy, M. Righetti defines the scrutinies in these terms:

> "The scrutinies are a complex of liturgical actions, whereby through the accompanying prayers, exorcisms, anointings, and renunciations of Satan, the Church attempts to purify the soul and body of the 'competens' of any possible demonic influence, in order to assure his fruitful reception of the grace of baptism.
>
> "The purpose of the scrutinies was not then, at least in the beginning, to verify the degree of his religious instruction or of his spiritual

progress, but to *scrutinize* himself (that is, to penetrate his own heart and to be assured that the mysterious action of God is working there) so as to be free of all domination by an impure spirit, with the understanding, of course, that this progressive liberation is the fruit of faith."[2]

It was not until the end of the fourth century that the Church, faced with the rapid influx of converts, gave a definite shape or organization to these scrutinies. The question which concerns us is the practice of the scrutinies before this organization.

Hippolytus of Rome gives us the most ancient testimony regarding the scrutinies. He clearly distinguishes two types of exorcisms which correspond to the two periods of the catechumenate as presented in his *Apostolic Tradition*. The first type is connected with the period of catechetical instruction which took place in church, and in an atmosphere of prayer:

"When the teacher has finished the catechesis, the catechumens pray by themselves, apart from the faithful."[3]

"After the prayer, when the teacher imposes hands on the catechumens, he prays for them and then dismisses them. Whoever teaches, whether cleric or lay person, should do this."[4]

This imposition of hands after the catechesis is a kind of exorcism linked to hearing the Word and to prayer.[5]

The second type of exorcism that Hippolytus attests to are *daily exorcisms* which culminated in a more solemn exorcism celebrated by the bishop. These daily exorcisms took place during the time of immediate preparation for Baptism, which in the time of Hippolytus lasted for one week.[6]

> "From the time when they are set apart, they are exorcised every day by imposition of hands. As the day of their baptism approaches, the bishop will exorcise each one of them to assure that they have been purified. If one of them has not acted in an upright manner or is impure, he will be dismissed, because he has not listened to the word faithfully and the Evil One cannot always go unnoticed.
> "Those who are to be baptised will be instructed to bathe and wash on Thursday. On Friday they are to fast. On Saturday the bishop will gather in one place all those who will receive baptism. He will ask them to kneel and pray, while imposing hands over them. The bishop will order all evil spirits to depart and never to return. When he has finished with the exorcism, the bishop will breathe on their faces. After signing them with the cross on the forehead, the ears, and nostrils, he will then have them stand."[7]

The meaning of the exorcism is clear: its purpose is to scrutinize the heart of the candidate to discern his purity and worthiness for Baptism.

A century earlier, Justin already mentioned that there was a time of prayer and communal fasting to ask for forgiveness of sins, although he does not mention exorcisms.[8]

Thus, besides the exorcisms, (followed by a breathing on the candidates and signations—which seem to recall the rite of ephpheta), there are also prayers (on their knees), purifications and fasts. As was prayer, fasting was also traditional among the Jewish people as a means for chasing away evil spirits (Matt.17:21). The earliest Christians also recognized it as a privileged means for preparing for baptism, as confirmed by the *Didache* (7,4) at the end of the first century and by Tertullian in the middle of the second.[9] Likewise, the breathing on the candidates and the signations also conveyed the idea of exorcism.

As another rite of exorcism we may include the anointing with oil during the course of the Easter Vigil after the renunciation of Satan and just before the Baptism. Hippolytus calls this "the oil of exorcism," and that the one administering it should say the words, "May every evil spirit depart from you." [10]

In the middle of the third century, Cyprian also speaks of exorcists who "by their human words, and aided by divine power, flagellate, burn, and torture the Devil." [11] He confirms the existence of exorcisms, but also points out that their power is not to be equated with that of Baptism. In the battle with the devil which is characteristic of the entire process of Christian initiation, the exorcisms do have their role to play. But they cannot free man from the radical grasp of the devil. Only Baptism can effect this total deliverance from the devil.

Fourth and Fifth Centuries

In the fourth and fifth centuries, the exorcisms and associated practices continued to occupy an important place in the process of Christian initiation—in Rome,

in the East, and in Africa. But since during this period
the time of the catechumenate was reduced to the
Lenten period, it is there that we will find the
exorcisms most generally celebrated. And with the
passage of time, there developed a number and
variety of rites of exorcism.

During this period we can distinguish at least three
types of exorcism: (1) The daily exorcisms of those in
immediate preparation for Baptism, administered by
clerics;[12] (2) the major scrutinies which marked off
the principal stages of immediate preparation for
Baptism and which always included a solemn exorcism; and (3) the exorcism which was celebrated
during the Easter vigil.[13]

The ceremony of these rites of exorcism developed
in such a way as to highlight the casting-off of the old
self. The candidate, for example, was covered only by
a scant costume (such as a hair shirt) and stood in his
bare feet on an animal skin. He had to extend his arms
wide, as in an attitude of prayer, with his gaze
lowered.[14] At the moment of the major exorcism, with
the anointing, the candidate was completely naked.

We must be aware that when the Fathers of the
Church speak of exorcisms, they are doing so in a very
wide sense, including all of the practices we have
mentioned thus far: prayer, fasting, breathing on the
candidates, as well as reading from the Scriptures.[15]

All these rites express the conflict which goes on
within the heart of the convert between Christ and
Satan, who tries to block the candidate's path to God
and keep him in his clutches. All the Lenten catechumenal exercises attempt to progressively disengage
the soul from the influence of the devil.

In short, the scrutinies were never meant to be an

examination of the candidate's knowledge of the truths of faith—which is precisely how they did develop in the West several centuries later. Rather they were an ensemble of liturgical actions and rites designed to free the candidate's heart from domination by evil spirits. At the same time, the scrutinies gave the Church a chance to confirm the proper disposition of those about to be baptized.

The Fathers used a number of images to illustrate the significance of the scrutinies:the refining of gold,[16] putting a house in good order,[17] the pleading of a case,[18] and combat in the arena.[19]

Because the early Church was well aware of the fact that these scrutinies were not magical rites, they always were careful to examine the active participation of the candidates as well as their verbal responses to the scrutinies. In this regard St. Augustine paid very close attention to the fervent attitudes of the candidates manifested throughout all the Lenten services and exercises—"their punctuality in gathering for the regular reunions, their ardor, the interest with which they listen," and everything which contributed to their "putting away the old man" and donning the clothes of the new.[20] He exhorts them not be be content with just going through the ceremony of the rites:

> "What we begin in you by exhortations made in the name of your Redeemer, bring to completion by the appropriate examination of your soul and by heartfelt contrition. By our prayers and exorcisms, we engage in combat against the deceitful ruses of that old enemy. On your part, you must persevere in prayer and contrition of heart in order to be freed from the clutches of darkness and transport-

ed into the kingdom of His brilliant light. This, now, is your task. It is also ours. We heap upon the head of your enemy all the anathemas which his heinous crimes deserve. On your part, give yourselves completely to this glorious battle, so that with the proper horror you may renounce all your contacts with him . . . I ask of you only one thing: to direct your will completely to your Redeemer who will come to deliver you."[21]

Developments from the Sixth Century

Beginning with the sixth century the number and variety of the scrutinies proliferates, but in the process their deep significance becomes obliterated. At first, they sometimes were celebrated on the third, fourth, and fifth Sundays of Lent. In addition, the scrutinies of the third Sunday of Lent were accompanied by an anointing. But after a while, the number of scrutinies increased to seven, but all celebrated within the course of one week. During the two centuries which followed, the catechumenate was no longer lived seriously by its members, most of whom were now infants, and as a result, the scrutinies simply lost contact with reality—the reality of a lived journey in faith and of progressive growth in the Christian life. By the year 800, the celebration of the seven scrutinies was telescoped into one, and even in that one celebration, the rite of exorcism had disappeared.[22]

The Meaning of the Scrutinies Today

With an understanding of how the scrutinies developed throughout the early history of the Church, we can now turn to the scrutinies as presented in the *RCIA*. The first thing we notice is that the *RCIA* mirrors the most ancient practice of the Church by distinguishing two types of exorcisms: those celebrated during the catechumenate and those celebrated for the elect in the period of enlightenment (Lent).

Exorcisms during the Catechumenate

The catechumens "should be eager, then to take part in the Liturgy of the Word and to receive blessings and sacramentals" (*RCIA*, 12). "By suitable liturgical rites, Mother Church cleanses them little by little, and strengthens them with God's blessing" (*RCIA*, 19,3).

The catechumens are purified by what the RCIA calls the"first exorcisms" or the "minor exorcisms." In distinction to the exorcisms during the Lenten scrutinies, these catechumenal exorcisms are in a positive deprecative (and not imperative) form. Their purpose is to "show the catechumens the true nature of the spiritual life as a battle between flesh and spirit," and to "underline both the importance of self-denial in order to gain the blessings of the Kingdom of God and the continuing need of God's help" (*RCIA*, 101). The new Rite presents the exorcisms in the form of orations and prayers which can accompany a celebration of the Word.

Within this first type we should also include the breathing on the candidates, which is part of the rite of entrance into the catechumenate (*RCIA*, 79).

During the catechumenal period the Rite stipulates that the candidates are strengthened by God's blessing. In pronouncing this blessing over each candidate, the Church manifests God's love to the catechumens as well as the Church's sincere concern for them. Thus, although "they still lack the grace of the sacraments, they may receive from the Church the spirit, joy, and peace to continue their work and spiritual journey" (*RCIA*, 102).

Exorcisms during the Lenten Period

During the period of the baptismal retreat, the purification of minds and hearts continues in a more intense fashion. It is within this context that the Church calls for the celebration of the scrutinies.

The purpose of the scrutinies is clearly stated by the new Rite: "The scrutinies . . . have a two-fold purpose: revealing anything that is weak, defective, or sinful in the hearts of the elect, so that it may be healed; and revealing what is upright, strong, and holy, so that it may be strengthened. The scrutinies are intended to free them from sin and the devil and to give them strength in Christ, who is the way, the truth, and the life for his chosen ones" (*RCIA*, 25,1). Their purpose, then, "is mainly spiritual . . . The scrutinies are intended to purify the catechumens' minds and hearts, to strengthen them against temptation, to purify their intentions, and to make firm their decision, so that they remain more closely united with Christ and make progress in their efforts to love God more deeply" (*RCIA,* 154).

Following St. Augustine, the new Rite underlines the necessity of the candidates' *participation* in this work of enlightenment and purification: "The mature candidates should have the intention of arriving at an intimate knowledge of Christ and his Church, and they are expected to progress in sincere self-knowledge, in a serious appraisal of self, and in true penance" (*RCIA,* 155).

The scrutinies include the rites of solemn exorcism.[23] When the *RCIA* was still in its experimental stage, the earlier drafts called these exorcisms the "major" exorcisms, and they were presented in the traditional imperative form—that is, they addressed Satan himself, and ordered him to depart. Unfortunately the revised final text of the *RCIA* has cast them in the more simple deprecative form.

By the rite of exorcism, the Church instructs the elect in the mystery of Christ, who brings deliverance from sin and the influence of the devil. They are strengthened in their spiritual journey and their hearts are prepared to receive the gifts of the Lord (*RCIA,* 156).

Normally there are three scrutines celebrated in the course of the Lenten period. They are celebrated in the presence of the community so that "the faithful too may benefit from the liturgy of the scrutinies and join in praying for the elect," (*RCIA,* 158). And they are celebrated, hopefully, on the third, fourth, and fifth Sundays of Lent, during the course of the Mass. The readings for these Sundays are the traditional texts for the Mass of the Scrutinies: the Samaritan Woman, the man born blind, and the raising of Lazarus.[24] These texts should always be used, even if for pastoral reasons the celebration of the rite must be shifted to a weekday (*RCIA*, 159). For the orations and special prayers for these Masses of the scrutinies, see *RCIA* 377, 381 and 385.

The three scrutinies are celebrated successively in order that the candidates may "progress in the understanding of sin and in the desire for salvation" (*RCIA*, 157). In order to realize this twofold purpose, the catechumens are instructed gradually in the mystery of sin, from which the whole world and each person desires to be redeemed, and thus be saved from its present and future effects" (*RCIA*, 157). They also "fill their minds with the meaning of Christ the Redeemer. He is the living water (see Gospel story of the Samaritan woman), light (see the Gospel story of the man born blind), resurrection and life (see Gospel story of the raising of Lazarus)" (*RCIA*, 157).

Only for the most serious reasons can the bishop dispense with one or even two of the scrutinies (*RCIA*, 66).

The Structure of the Scrutinies

THE structure of all three scrutinies is identical (*RCIA*, 160-180), but the text of the prayers does vary for each. (Unlike the scrutinies as celebrated prior to the RCIA, there is no longer any distinction between prayers said over men and those said over women.) The structure is rather simple and consists of four parts:

Liturgy of the Word: The suggested readings are indicated in *RCIA* 376, 380 and 384. To these one could add several passages from the epistles which deal with the fight against Satan, such as Eph 6:18-20, or 1 Peter 5:6-11. The homily then follows.

Period of Silent Prayer (RCIA, 160, and parallel paragraphs in second and third scrutinies): The elect and their sponsors come before the celebrant, who first invites the faithful to pray silently for the elect that they may receive the spirit of repentance, an understanding of sin, and the true freedom of children of God. He then invites the elect to pray in silence, and to express their spirit of repentance by a bodily gesture such as bowing or kneeling.

Prayer for the Elect (RCIA, 163 and 378): This consists of intentions made on behalf of the candidates, with a refrain after each intention. During this prayer the godparents place their right hands on the right shoulders of their godchildren.

Exorcism (RCIA, 164 and 379, plus parallels): The exorcism within the rite of the scrutinies consists of three parts. First the celebrant, with hands joined, says

an oration which is addressed to God. The he lays
hands in silence on each candidate. Finally, the
celebrant addresses an oration to Christ while extending his hands over the elect.

Some Points for Reflection

THIS author's experience with Christian initiation has been in a culture which affords an important place to the reality of spirits and the constant battle against evil spirits. From this perspective, it seems that the new Rite tends to minimalize if not the reality, at least the fashion of speaking about Satan. We would recommend taking full advantage of the possibility that the new Rite gives for celebrating the minor exorcisms during the period of the catechumenate.

In cultures and areas which take seriously a belief in evil spirits or the devil, it will be necessary to review and adopt the notion of and celebration of the scrutinies to be more in keeping with their experience with evil.

It is important that people understand the meaning of the time for silent prayer just before the exorcism. It might also be a good idea to include within this time an examiniation of conscience.

The supplications and intercessions for the elect would be even more effective if they were offered by the godparents while at the same time imposing their hands over their godchildren. To these intercessions *for* the elect, might it not also be desirable to add an intention offered *by* the elect themselves as an expression of their need and willingness for conversion?

The exorcisms of the scrutinies should be in the *imperative* form, rather than in the deprecative form as they are now.

One question we must pose is how can we better

express the active participation of the elect in this divine action of exorcism—that the elect are not just passive recipients? The Mossi tribe furnishes us with one example. At the time the exorcism is celebrated, in between the two orations by the celebrant, the elect chant a song in which they ask God for protection from the devil. This is comparable to the pleas made by the sick for Christ to heal them, as we see continually in the New Testament. In another tribe, in place of this chant there is a dialogue between the priest and the elect.

We must also be careful to find gestures which are most expressive within the given culture of just what exorcism is. In certain areas of Africa, instead of imposing hands on the head of the elect, the celebrant places both his hands on the back of the elect, who kneels down and bends forward. This particular gesture is commonly recognized among these people as the proper position for chasing away evil spirits. Among the people of the Gourmantché tribe, the celebrant, after the first oration, turns to face the four major points of the compass as an expression of faith in Christ's cosmic victory over all evil spirits.

In implementing the rite of the scrutinies, and particularly the exorcisms, care should be taken to highlight the role of the Holy Spirit. In this regard the new Rite is very deficient. The first oration makes no mention at all of the Holy Spirit, while the second only alludes to Him in passing. Among the Gourmantché, there is an explicit calling upon the Holy Spirit immediately after the exorcism. The elect respond "Amen" to each invocation chanted by the celebrant. During this time, the sponsors place their hands on the shoulders of the candidates.

Normally, the anointing should take place during the Easter Vigil, or at least sometime on Holy Saturday (*RCIA*, 206). But some prefer to join the anointing with one of the scrutinies, for example, the third in order to give it more solemnity, or with one of the rites of transition during the catechumenate (as presented in Chapter 2).

In this chapter we have looked at one of the rites proper to the Lenten period of enlightenment. We now turn to a rite closely associated with the scrutinies: the Presentations.

Notes

[1]For information on the history of the scrutinies, consult Michel Dujarier, *The History of the Catechumenate, The First Six Centuries,* New York: William H. Sadlier, Inc., 1979; A. Dondeyne, "La discipline des scrutins dans l'Eglise latine avant Charlemagne," in *RHE,* 28 (1932), pp. 5-33, 751-787; H. Leclercq, "Scrutins," article in *DACL* IV, 1037-1052; A. Chavasse, "Le carême romain et les scrutins prébapismaux," in *RSR,* 48 (1960), pp. 227-240; and J.M. Hansens, "Scrutins et sacramentaires," *Gregorianum,* 41 (1960), pp. 692-700.

[2]Mario Righetti, *Manuale di storia liturgica,* Vol. IV, Milan: Editrice Ancora, 1950-56, p. 55.

[3]*AT,* 18.

[4]*Ibid.,* 19.

[5]Theodotus (2nd century) confirms the significance of imposition of hands as an exorcism. See Clement of Alexandria's *Excerpta ex Theodoto,* edited with translation, introduction, and notes by Robert Pierce Casey, London: The Christophers, 1934.

[6]Cf. Michel Dujarier, *Le Parrainage des adultes,* pp. 231-232.

[7]*AT,* 20.

[8]See Chapter III, p.82; Jusin, *I Apol.* 61,2.

[9]Tertullian, *De Baptismo,* 20,1.

[10]*AT,* 21.

[11]Cyprian, *Epistle* 69,15.

[12]*Pilgrimage of Egeria,* 48; *Catecheses* of John Chrysostom, II,12.

[13]Cyril of Jerusalem, *Catecheses,* 20,3.

[14]Theodore of Mopsuestia, *Catechetical Homilies,* XII, introduction and paragraphs 17-25.

[15]Cyril of Jerusalem, *PG* 33,349.

[16]Cyril of Jerusalem, *Procatechesis,* 9.

[17]St. John Chrysostom, *Catecheses,* 2,11-12.

[18]Theodore of Mopsuestia, *Homily* 12, 17-25.

[19]Augustine, *Sermon* 216,6.

[20]Augustine, *De fide et operibus,* VI,9.

[21]Augustine, *Sermon* 216, 6-7.

[22]See A. Chavasse's article in *RSR,* 35, pp. 375-380.

[23]For more information on exorcisms, consult J. Forget, "Exorcisme," in *DTC* V, 1762-1780; J. Danielou, "Exorcisme" in *DS,* IV, 1995-2004; R. Beraudy, "Les exorcismes prébaptismaux," in *Assemblées du Seigneur,* ancienne serie, n. 30, *Troisième dimanche du carême,* 1963), pp.

7-17; R. Beraudy, "Scrutinies and Exorcisms," in Concilium, 22, 1967, pp. 57-61. It is surprising to read in this article that " . . . the exorcism is very logically a unilateral act of God with which the person is only passively associated." The first half of Vol. 22 in the Concilium series deals with Christian initiation from theological, catechetical, liturgical, biblical, and historical perspectives. Note also the article by M. Dujarier on Sponsorship, pp. 45-50 (translator's note).

[24]These readings are all from the "A" Cycle of the lectionary. For more on this subject, see Thierry Maertens, " History and Function of the Three Great Pericopes: The Samaritan Woman, The Man Born Blind, and the Raising of Lazarus," in Concilium, 22, 1967, pp. 51-56.

Chapter 5
The Presentations

THE period of enlightenment, the candidate's immediate preparation for Baptism, is marked by the celebration of two rites: the Scrutinies, which we treated in the previous chapter, and the Presentations.

By "Presentations" we are referring to the celebrations in which the candidates are presented with the Creed and with the Lord's prayer. The Creed and the Lord's Prayer are the formulas which have carried the Church's traditions of faith and of prayer from one generation of believers to the next.[1]

During the fourth and fifth centuries there developed the practice of celebrating the Presentation of the Creed and the Our Father within the Lenten period. This was followed a short time later by the ceremony of repetition, in which the candidates demonstrated their knowledge of these two traditions.

In restoring the Presentations among the rites of the catechumenate, the RCIA offers us a valuable instrument for highlighting the essential initiatory dimension of the communal journey towards baptism.

It is precisely because the Presentations can help manifest the initiatory dimension of the catechumenal journey that we will devote this chapter to their study.

Historical Overview

ALTHOUGH the Presentations as we know them did not find their way into the catechumenal process until rather late (the fourth century) they manifest an important characteristic of Christian initiation present since the earliest beginnings. Before looking at the traditions which are presented to the candidates in the new Rite, let us remark that "tradition" is a constitutive dimension of the motherhood of the Church— tradition conceived not simply as some*thing* transmitted, but first and foremost as the *action* of transmitting, an action which involves and flows from the very heart of the life of the community. Before it becomes a "thing," tradition is primarily an *action*.

For people who live in what we sometimes term "primitive" cultures, tradition is clearly recognized as the living link which attaches them to their ancestors. It functions as the sacred milieu in which the individual is formed and informed from cradle to grave. Tribal initiation rites provide a very clear example of this. By the secret language which the young ones learn, by the revelations to them, by their recitation of sacred texts, by the new names they receive, by the assistance of the elders, and by the knowledge they acquire through their own personal experience, those who are initiated are integrated into the social life of the tribe. They become adults and are inserted into the living tradition of the community. To honor and respect the *tradition* of the community is understood both as a witness of fidelity to ancestors and a guarantee of a successful life.

Unfortunately in a highly technical, mobile, and pluralistic society such as that of the United States, tradition does not occupy the primary position it does in many other cultures. And yet it is no less an important factor in the life of the Church, especially when Christian initiation is concerned.[2]

Tradition and the Church

In his first letter to the Corinthians, St. Paul treats faith in the risen Lord in terms of a dialectic between "faith received" and "faith transmitted," or between "faith which is kept" and "faith which is proclaimed":

> "Brothers, I want to remind you of the gospel I preached to you, which you received and in which you stand firm. You are being saved by it at this very moment if you hold fast to it as I preached it to you. Otherwise you have believed in vain. I handed on to you first of all what I myself received . . . In any case, whether it be I or they, this is what we preach and this is what you believe."[3]

The same is true for the Eucharist: "I received from the Lord what I handed on to you . . . "[4]

This understanding of "tradition" as the heart of the community, especially of the family community (cf. 2 Tim 1:5), is both the basis and the guarantee of authentic faith.

St. Irenaeus developed this theme of tradition to an unparalleled degree, and which future generations of theologians would echo for centuries.

> "The Church is the recipient of the kerygma and the faith of the apostles. Although it now

stretches throughout the world, she guards it carefully, as if all who hold it are members of the same household, and it is believed unanimously, as if all were of the same heart and soul, and it proclaims it with one voice, and she teaches and transmits it with one mouth. The language of the world may be different, but the power of tradition is always one and the same."[5]

"Thus, as for the tradition of the Apostles, manifested throughout the world, it is in the Church that it is perceived by all those who wish to see the truth."[6]

"We guard carefully the faith we have received from the Church. For through the action of the Spirit of God, this precious deposit, enclosed within such an excellent vase, is ceaselessly rejuvenated, and in turn rejuvenates the very vase which contains it."[7]

It is within the perspective of Christian initiation conceived as a progressive entrance into the living tradition of the community that the liturgical ceremonies called the "traditions"—and what the RCIA calls the "Presentations"—developed.

In the fourth and fifth centuries, there were only two traditions presented to the candidates: the Creed and the Lord's Prayer. As we shall shortly see, the Presentations of these two traditions were more than just a ceremonial rite, but a process lived and experienced with all the adults preparing for Baptism.

In the sixth and seventh centuries, the same ceremonies for the Presentations existed in the liturgy— but *only* in the liturgy. By this time, infant Baptism was the norm instead of the exception, and so the Presen-

138

tations lost their important aspect of lived experience. It is within this context of artificial ritualism that two other "traditions" found their way into the baptismal rite: the presentation of the Gospels, and, in Náples, the presentation of the Psalms.

The Presentation of the Creed

From the very beginning, Mother Church was always careful to hand down faithfully the treasure of her faith. Thus, according to the Fathers, the Church presented to the catechumens what they termed the "Rule of Faith" or "The Canon of Truth." This sacred deposit of faith was summarized in the format we today call the Creed, the formulation of which developed gradually during the first centuries of the Church's life.[8]

Historical evidence confirms that the Presentation of the Creed was celebrated in both the East and the West from the fourth century. It consisted of an instruction given by the bishop on the articles of the Creed, and was addressed to the elect who would be baptized at the next celebration of Easter. Normally, this instruction was conducted on the fifth Sunday of Lent, although in other places and times, it was celebrated on the third, fourth or sixth Sundays. Sometimes this catechesis extended over several days, as confirmed by a number of documents.[9]

The Creed was never presented to the elect in written form, but always orally, and candidates had to memorize it. A week later, they recited it publicly.

Cyril reflects the practice in Jerusalem of the mid-fourth century, when he says to the elect:

"Within these verses are contained all instruction in the faith. This is what I want you to retain verbatim, and which each of you must carefully recite, without writing it on paper, but by engraving it by memory in your hearts. Be careful that in reciting it, no cate-chumen hears what has been handed down to you. Keep this faith as the only provision you need for your journey all the rest of your life, and receive no other. See now, my brothers, and keep the traditions which you now receive and write them in bold letters within your hearts."[10]

At the end of the fourth century, Egeria describes the presentation and recitation of the traditions in these terms:

> "After five weeks of instructions (on the Scriptures) those preparing for the reception of Baptism receive the Creed. As with the Scriptures, the teaching of the Creed is ex-plained to them phrase by phrase, first in its literal meaning, and then in its spiritual meaning."

At the end of the seventh week of Lent,

> "the bishop's chair is placed at the rear of the apse, behind the altar. Then the candidates come forward one by one, the men with their godfathers, and the women with their god-mothers, and recite the Creed for the bishop."[11]

In Northern Africa, St. Augustine specifies the most essential aspect of the Presentations: they are not simply a matter of memorizing and reciting, but are the handing on of a faith which, through the work of the Holy Spirit, must lead not just to knowledge but to practice and continuous growth:

> "He who has called you to his kingdom and glory will grant that, when you have been regenerated by his grace and by the Holy Spirit, it will be written in your hearts, so that you may love what you believe and that, through love, faith may work in you and that you may become pleasing to the Lord God, the giver of all good things, not by fearing his punishment in a servile fashion, but by loving justice as true sons of God. This, therefore, is the Creed which has become familiar to you through Scripture and through ecclesiastical sermons. Under this brief formula the faithful must live and advance."[12]

The Presentation of the Lord's Prayer

Well before the institution of the ceremony of the Presentation of the Lord's Prayer, the Church had been careful to introduce catechumens to the uniqueness and originality of Christian prayer. This preoccupation of the early Church is exemplified in three fundamental works on the Our Father dating from the third century—all from African authors: Tertullian, Origen, and Cyprian.[13] For the presentation of the Creed, we possess numerous documents of the fourth and fifth centuries.

During these centuries, the Presentation of the Lord's Prayer took place at some time *after* the Presentation of the Creed. According to Augustine, the ceremony was celebrated on the sixth Sunday of

Lent, and the recitation took place on the morning of Holy Saturday. In many places this more formal recitation was reduced to a simple proclamation of the Our Father during the baptismal Mass.

The bishop confided the Lord's Prayer to the elect, and they had to be prepared to recite it from memory eight days later. The Lord's Prayer was understood as a prayer reserved to Christians, and *baptized* Christians at that. As Augustine said, "How can someone say 'Our Father' if he has not yet been born?"[14]

On the day of the Presentation, it was customary to explain to the elect the words of the Lord's Prayer as found in Mt. 6:7ff, which had just been proclaimed. We possess a number of such sermons[15] which stress that we receive this prayer from the Lord Jesus himself, handed down to us by his disciples.

Augustine was fond of emphasizing the place of the Lord's Prayer in the life of a Christian: "This prayer encourages you not just to learn to ask your Father in heaven for the things you want, but to learn also what you *should* want."[16] And in a homily on Matthew 5, he ties together beautifully the petitions of the Our Father and the beatitudes, thus uniting Christian prayer with Christian living.[17]

Theodore of Mopsuestia likewise insists on the necessary link between this prayer and the Christian's style of life:

> "Realizing that coupled with correct teaching and a sincere faith, we must also strive towards good living and good works, our blessed fathers handed on this prayer to those advancing toward the gift of baptism. By their exposition of the faith, they instruct us in correct teaching; and by this prayer they

help us to so order our lives that we may possess the perfection required from those who receive the gift of baptism, those who, while still here on earth, are counted among the citizens of a heavenly life."[18]

The Presentation of the Gospels

During the time when most of those presented for Baptism were no longer adults but infants, we see the appearance of a curious ceremony counted among the Presentations: the presentation of the Gospels. In Rome, the ceremony took place as follows: After the chanting of the Gradual, four deacons, accompanied by four acolytes each carrying a candle, processed solemnly with the four Gospels, which they placed at four corners of the altar. After the pope had read an invitatory, each of the deacons read the opening verses of the Gospels,[19] explaining at that moment the symbol of each evangelist—the man, the lion, the ox, and the eagle. Most likely, this ceremony, which was specifically intended for infants, was an attempt to compensate ritually for a catechesis which, in view of the very young age of the candidates, could not be realized.

It appears that this custom, the first traces of which we find in the Gelasian sacramentary dating back to the sixth century, was confined to western Europe.

In the seventh century, the three Presentations—first the Gospels, followed by the Creed and finally the Lord's Prayer—were celebrated on successive Sundays and were joined with the celebration of the three scrutinies. But in the eighth and ninth centuries, when the number of scrutinies had increased to seven, the three presentations were celebrated all together at the same time, in the course of the third scrutiny on the Wednesday before Passion Sunday.

Presentation of the Psalms

The ceremony of the presentation of the Psalms seems to have been limited to Naples. It took place on the third Sunday of Lent. This practice is attested to by a series of homilies from the mid-sixth century in which Bishop John the Mediocre invites the elect to learn by heart the 22nd Psalm, or at least Psalm 116— much shorter and therefore easier to memorize. Psalm 41 is also mentioned as a possibility.[20]

The Meaning of the Presentations

THE preliminary remarks in the *RCIA* can help us to understand the significance of the Presentations.

The Purpose of the Presentations

The Presentations, by which the Church transmits to the elect the ancient heritage of her faith and prayer, are intended to "enlighten" or "illuminate" the elect:

> "The profession of faith recalls the wonderful work of God for the salvation of man; it deepens the faith and joy of the elect. In the Lord's Prayer, they acknowledge more firmly the new spirit of sonship by which they will call God their Father, especially in the midst of the congregation assembled for the Eucharist" (*RCIA*, 25,2).

Thus, the Church transmits to the elect the very texts regarded from antiquity as the summary of her faith and prayer. But it would have been better if in the introduction, the *RCIA* had underscored more than it does the communal and living dimension of the *action* of tradition which is so essential to all initiation.

When to Celebrate?

The Presentations follow the celebration of the scrutinies and belong to the period of enlightenment and purification of the elect, which usually coincides with Lent.

The *RCIA* specifies that, unlike the scrutinies which are normally celebrated on Sunday, the Presentations are to be celebrated on a weekday. The Creed is given during the week following the first scrutiny; the Lord's Prayer during the week following the third scrutiny, or even on the morning of Holy Saturday (*RCIA,* 189).

It is difficult to see the logic of this prescription. If the presentations really are the visible sign of the official transmission of her family treasures which the Church makes to the elect, would it not be more sensible to celebrate them on a Sunday, before the entire assembled community? The RCIA itself seems to recognize this when it says that the Presentations are to be celebrated "in the presence of the community of the faithful" (182).

For pastoral reasons, the Presentations may be celebrated during the time of the catechumenate proper, in which case they fall under the category of rites celebrated during the stages of the catechumenate, or the "rites of transition." What are the pastoral situations which would call for this displacement of the presentations?

One such reason could be the lack of time to celebrate them during the Lenten period. The Rite already calls for the celebration of the three Scrutinies during this time. Anticipating the Presentations in the catechumenate period would also discourage a much less desirable solution: coupling the celebration of the Presentations with the Scrutinies, which would result in a liturgical hodgepodge.

In a more positive way, anticipating the Presentations can help to mark the passage from one stage of the catechumenate period to another, provided of course that the candidate has reached a sufficient stage in his/her faith in order to genuinely celebrate the Presentations. In this case, we suggest that the Presentation of the Lord's Prayer *precede* the Presentation of the Creed (thus reversing the normal order), which presupposes a more advanced knowledge of the faith.

We have already pointed out that the Presentations, so rich in significance themselves, lost all their pastoral value to the extent that the *liturgical* rite was not grounded either on an effective catechesis or on lived experience.

This observation is a lesson of history we must be well aware of if we hope at all to restore a genuine celebration of our traditions to the process of Christian initiation.

The Structure
of the Presentations

THE Presentations should be celebrated in the presence of the community of the *faithful*, in the course of a Mass if possible, and always with an appropriate Liturgy of the Word.

Presentation of the Creed

The Liturgy of the Word (RCIA, 185): The RCIA proposes the following texts. The first reading is from the Old Testament, (Deut. 6:1-7). The passage contains Israel's traditional profession of faith which is used by Jesus in Mk. 12:29-30. This text also enriches the rite of Presentation by alluding to the transmission of God's commandments, which every father must do for his children.

For the second reading the RCIA suggests either Rom. 10:8-13, the confession of faith of one who believes in God, or 1 Cor. 15:1-8a (or shortened to 1-4). The second text appears to be the better one, since it emphasizes the dialectic between faith transmitted and faith received.

For the Gospel, after having sung John 3:16 as an acclamation, the RCIA suggests Mt. 16:13-18, Peter's confession of faith in Jesus, or John 12:44-50, which highlights more the dimension of "tradition-reception" of God the Father to his Son, Jesus, and from Jesus to us.

In his homily, the celebrant explains the meaning

and importance of the Creed, not just as a summary of all the catechesis received up to this point, but also to prepare the candidate for the profession of the Creed at Baptism, and also so that through a proper understanding of the Creed, he may be able to be faithful to it for the rest of his life.

The Rite Itself (RCIA 186): The deacon invites the elect to come forward to receive from the Church her profession of faith. The celebrant then exhorts them to accept this tradition. The Creed—either the Apostles' or the Nicene—is then proclaimed by the celebrant alone, or better yet, by the entire community of the *faithful*—but not by the elect, who must *listen* to it.

The Prayer (RCIA, 187): The celebrant begins by inviting the community to pray for the elect. A period of silence then follows, and the celebrant concludes with an oration.

The Recitation: The elect do not recite the Creed at the ceremony of Presentation. The recitation can take place either on Holy Saturday morning or at the baptismal Mass.

The goal of the recitation is twofold: (1) to prepare the elect for their profession of faith, and (2) to instruct the elect in their duty to proclaim the Gospel.

The Liturgy of the Word for the rite of recitation begins with an appropriate song, followed by the readings: either Matt. 16:13-17 if this was not used at the rite of Presentation; or John 6:35,63-71; or perhaps Mark 7:31-37 if the rite of ephpheta will also be celebrated at this time. The homily then follows.

As just mentioned, the rite of ephpheta (*RCIA,* 202) can be inserted here, symbolizing the necessity of grace in order to be able to hear the Word of God and to profess it (*RCIA*, 200).

The celebrant then prays for the elect, after which they recite the Creed.

Presentation of the Lord's Prayer

It should be noted that, unlike the Presentation of the Creed, which occurs after the homily, the Presentation of the Lord's Prayer takes place in the proclamation of the Gospel (*RCIA*, 191).

Readings: For the reading from the Old Testament, the RCIA suggests Hosea 11:16,3-4, showing how God leads us by the reins of love.

There are two possibilities for the responsorial psalm: Ps. 22:1-6, with v. 1 as the refrain, a statement of God's protective guidance; or Ps. 102:1-2, 8, 10-13, 18, with v. 13 as the refrain, which compares God's love for us to a father's love for his children.

For the second reading, the RCIA gives two alternatives from the Pauline epistles: Romans 8:14-17, 26-27 or Galatians 4:4-7, both of which reveal that it is the Spirit who empowers us to call God as "Father."

This theme is picked up by the Gospel acclamation "You have received the spirit which makes us God's children, and in that Spirit we call God 'our Father' " (Rom. 8:15).

The Rite Itself (RCIA, 191): The Lord's Prayer is presented to the elect in the proclamation of the Gospel. After the Gospel acclamation, the deacon invites the elect to step forward. The celebrant then urges them to listen attentively to how the Lord taught his disciples to pray. Matt. 6:9-13 is then proclaimed. In the homily which follows, the celebrant explains the meaning and importance of the Lord's Prayer.

The Prayer (RCIA, 192): The celebrant invites the faithful to pray for the elect. After a pause for silent prayer, the celebrant concludes by extending his hands over the elect and praying for them out loud.

The format of the Presentation of the Lord's Prayer differs in another respect from that of the Creed in that the rite calls for no recitation of the Lord's Prayer by the elect. From antiquity, this prayer was considered the exclusive prerogative not of the whole Christian community, but of those who, through Baptism, have already received the spirit of God's adopted children. Therefore, while the elect received this tradition previous to their Baptism, they could only listen to it and not yet pronounce it. Only as baptized neophytes will they be able to pray it themselves, along with the other baptized members of the community at the first celebration of the Eucharist in which they participate.

Other Rites of Presentation?: We mentioned earlier that in the sixth century the Church celebrated a rite of presentation of the Gospels. While this rite no longer exists autonomously in the RCIA, we can nevertheless consider the stage of entrance into the catechumenate as supplying the candidate with a solemn "presentation" of the Word of God. Recall that during the ceremony of the rite of entrance, the celebrant addressed the candidates on the dignity of the Word of God as proclaimed in and heard by the Church. Then followed the solemn procession and enthronement of the Bible. The candidates then par-

ticipated in the Liturgy of the Word for the first time
(*RCIA*, 92). Finally, the candidates were presented with
a book of the Gospels, a New Testament, or the Bible.
What we have in effect here is a rite of presentation of
the Word of God, although this is not called as such
by the new Rite, nor is it counted among the rites
which make up the Presentations properly speaking.

The new Rite does not indicate any other rites of
presentation. But as we will see in the next section of
this chapter, it would be both fitting and beneficial to
consider the possibility of presenting to the candidates certain key passages of the New Testament.
These they could learn by heart and keep as texts
which can guide them long after their initiation and
throughout their entire lives.

While there is no rite of presentation of the Psalms
(as there was in the sixth century), the RCIA does
emphasize the Psalms as particularly appropriate in
processionals and recessionals. This does, however,
presuppose that the catechumens have received an
initiation into praying the psalms.

Finally, it is surprising that in Chapter 5 of the
RCIA,which deals with the initiation of children of
catechetical age, there is no mention of the Presentations. Surely just as much as adults, children need to
benefit from the richness of these ceremonies so
expressive of the communal reality of Christian life.

Points for Reflection

It is a real cause for joy that the ancient ceremonies of the Presentations have been restored in the RCIA, because in a very concrete way they manifest two essential convictions of the Church: first, the Church is a community which faithfully hands down from one generation to the next the treasure of its faith and life; and secondly, initiation is entrance into a living community from which we receive everything we need to transform and inspire our new life.

The very richness of this type of ceremony invites us to develop and expand several elements which the new Rite does not seem to stress nearly as much as it should.

Needed Emphasis on the Act of Transmission

A simple recitation of the Creed by the priest or the proclamation of the Lord's Prayer in Matt. 6:9-13 is just not expressive enough of the *act* of transmission—all the emphasis seems to lie on the "what," not on the "who" or the "how." As an example of what can be done to highlight these important agents of the transmission of faith (which the new Rite risks making appear secondary), we cite the practice of the Mossi tribe in presenting one of the traditions:

First of all, to establish a proper setting and atmosphere, the minister invites all the faithful to be seated while the elect remain standing. At this point, the candidates express their desire to deepen their initiation through a song or chant.

The president then sits down and addreses the candidates at some length and in a lively, spontaneous manner, explaining to them the meaning and consequences of the rite. The celebrant is careful to use many concrete signs and gestures, and to dialogue with the candidates. The rest of the community interrupts with acclamations and responses. Then, in order to make it very clear to the candidates that he is acting in union with all of the community (demonstrated also by the participation in the rite of the representative members of the community—organizers, catechists, etc.), the celebrant calls the faithful to gather around him, to profess the Creed or pray the Lord's Prayer. The celebrant is also careful to thank the faithful for sharing the traditions with the elect.

The elect demonstrate their reception of the traditions by repeating them phrase by phrase, and by appropriate gesture. After being presented the Word of God, for example, the candidates come forward and place their hands and forehead face down on the opened Bible. The elect then join with the faithful in a song of joy and praise.

Need to Celebrate the Presentations as Distinct Rites of Initiation.

Care must be taken that the celebration of the Presentations is not subsumed in any other liturgical ceremony which could then minimalize their importance.

In many places it has been customary to attach the Presentation of the Word of God to the first scrutiny, the Presentation of the Creed to the second scrutiny, and the Presentation of the Lord's Prayer to the third scrutiny. But this makes it very difficult to center the readings and the celebration on one clear theme.

In order to avoid needless multiplication of celebrations, it would be better to develop the Presentation of the Word of God as part of the rite of Entrance into the Catechumenate whereby the candidate is given access to the Word of God proclaimed in the Church.

An additional possibility would be to combine the Presentations of the Creed and the Lord's Prayer in one ceremony, centered on the theme of "tradition." There is also the possibility of dropping one of the three scrutinies.

The easiest solution, however, appears to be this. Instead of celebrating the Presentations during the Lenten period of enlightenment, anticipate their celebration during the catechumeante period. The presentations would thus become "transitional rites" celebrated to mark the progress of the candidates through the various stages and levels of the catechumenate. The Presentation of the Word of God could be celebrated as part of the rite of Entrance into the Catechumenate, marking the candidate's passage from the level of precatechesis to catechesis. The Lord's Prayer could be presented to mark the passage from the first year of the catechumenate to the second. The Creed could then be presented to mark the catechumen's passage from the second to the third year.

Presentation of Key New Testament Passages

Simply as an example of this possibility which we mentioned earlier, we might look at the practice which has emerged in Bobo-Dioulasso:[21]

During the Lenten period, the elect learn three

passages of the New Testament which summarize the three Christian essentials: faith (the prologue of John's Gospel); hope (the Beatitudes), and love (the hymn in 1 Cor. 13). Moreover, memorization of these texts introduced a needed balance to the former practice of having the candiates memorize only the Ten Commandments.

By the end of the Lenten period, in which many of the customary tribal rites of initiation were invested with a Christian significance by introducing them into the catechumenal rites, the candidates had matured and were ready to integrate themselves as active members of the family of the Church. Thus, in the presence of the bishop, the elders, and all the members of the community, the elect proclaimed their memorized texts in the course of a solemn ceremony.

Attempts such as the one described above should encourage us to study more closely the kind of texts which could enrich such a rite of presentation. For example, we might want to include the three Pauline hymns which summarize in a marvelous way the Christian view of world history from the perspective of the life of the Trinity (Ephes. 1:3-14); our faith in the incarnation and redemption of Christ (Phil. 2:6-11); and our faith in the universal primacy of Christ (Col. 1:15-20).

These texts could even become more useful if they could be put to song and accompanied by gestures.

A Practical Problem

In all of our discussions about the power, significance, and richness of the presentations, we must be aware of a very common problem: in reality, most catechumens learn and recite the Creed and the Our Father in the very first weeks of their formation. Because of this, the rite of Presentation of these two texts loses a lot of its effectiveness and power when it is deferred to much later—in fact almost to the end of their formation. What can we do about this?

One solution we have already mentioned: celebrate the Presentation of the Lord's Prayer at the end of the first year of the catechumenate, and that of the Creed at the end of the second year. The Lenten period could then be utilized for the presentation of key New Testament texts as mentioned above. Another text which might be presented in the Lenten period could be 1 John 4:7-16, which summarizes well our faith in God, who is Love, in his incarnate Son, Jesus Christ, in the Spirit, and in our life of union with God in the love of our brothers and sisters.

If the Our Father is presented early in the formation period, care should be taken that the candidates do not see it as just another Scripture text. It would be helpful if the Our Father could be presented within a session devoted to initiating the catechumens to Christian prayer.

Care should also be taken that the Creed not be learned all in one session, or as one block of material, but gradually throughout the extended formation time. This is precisely why we suggest that if the two traditions are anticipated, the Creed should come *after* the Lord's Prayer.

As we close this chapter, we sense more acutely both the richness and the demands of the Presentations. And this richness will be incalculable when we succeed in accomplishing all the research and work necessary for the establishment of a genuinely initia-

tory catechumenate, where the community faithfully
hands down to its new members its beliefs, its way of
life, and its hope.

Notes

[1] The choice of the term "presentations" in the English translation of the RCIA is somewhat unfortunate, since it makes no reference either to *what* is being presented or to *how* it is presented. The French term is much better: the "Traditions," thus referring not only to the content (the traditions of the Church) but also to the means—by tradition, that is by handing down. While we prefer the term "traditions" we will continue to refer to this rite as the "presentations" so as not to introduce any unnecessary confusion (translator's note).

[2] Cf. Raymond F. Refoulé , "Tradition, régle de foi et écriture," in Tertullian's *Traité de la préscription contre les hérétiques,"* in *Sources chrétiennes,* 46, pp. 45-66; also, A. Lauras, "Saint Léon le grand et la tradition," in *RSR,* 48, 1960; pp. 166-184, where the author highlights the double dimension of tradition as rule of faith and rule of life.

[3] 1 Cor. 15:1-3:11; from *The New American Bible,* Catholic Publishers Incorporated, 1971.

[4] 1 Cor. 11:23 *(NAB).*

[5] Irenaeus, *Adv. Her.,* 1, 10, 2.

[6] *Ibid.,* III,3,1.

[7] *Ibid.,* III,24,1.

[8] For information on the history of the formation of the Creed, see *Lumiére et Vie,* 2, February, 1952, and especially the article by P. Camelot, pp. 61-80.

[9] Among the principle catecheses on the Creed we mention here only some of the more accessible: Augustine, *The Easter Sermons,* translated by Philip Thomas Weller, Washington, D.C.: The Catholic University of America Press, 1955, sermons 212, 213, 214 *(De symbolo),* 215. *Sources chrétiennes,* vol. 116 offers an excellent introduction to Augustine's treatment of the Creed in the Easter sermons. Ambrose, *On the Mysteries,* translated by T. Thompson, edited by J.J. Srawley, New York: Macmillan, 1919; paragraph 46 deals with the Creed. Rufinus, *PL* 21, 335f. Leo the Great, *Homily on the Tradition of the Creed;* the text of this sermon is an exhortation to the catechumens before the reception of Baptism, during which Leo hands on the tradition of the Creed. While there are several easily available French translations (notably the *Admonition pour la tradition du symbole,* in *Sources chrétiennes,* 200, pp. 294 ff) the only extant English translation is found in Wilson, *The Gelasian Sacramentary,* Oxford: 1894. St. Caesar of Arles, *Sermons,* translated by Sister Mary Magdeleine Muller, OSF, vol 1 (sermons 1-80),

New York: Fathers of the Church, Inc., 1956; see sermons 9 through 12, pages 54-74, especially sermon 9: "The beginning of an explanation or instruction on the Creed." Cyril of Jerusalem: Beginning with the sixth catechesis and through to catechesis 18, Cyril develops an extended catechesis which parallels the tenets of the Creed. Theodore of Mopsuestia, *Commentary on the Nicene Creed*, Catechetical Homilies 1-10.

[10]Cyril of Jerusalem, *Catecheses*, V,12.

[11]*Pilgrimage of Egeria*, 46.

[12]Augustine, *Sermon* 212,2, quoted from *Augustine: Sermons on the Liturgical Seasons*, translated by Sr. Mary Sarah Muldowney, RSM, New York: The Fathers of the Church, Inc., 1959.

[13]Lengthy extracts from these three works can be found in Adalbert Hamman's, *Le Pater expliqué par les Pères*, Paris: Editions Franciscaines, nouvelle édition, 1962.

[14]Augustine, *Sermon* 59,7.

[15]Among the most accessible we may list: Augustine, *Sermon 59*, "On the Lord's Prayer." Ambrose, *The Sacraments*, V,4:18-30; and VI,3,4,5. John Cassian, *The First Conference of Abbot Isaac:* On Prayer, XVIII-XXIV, in *The Conferences of John Cassian*. St. Peter Chrysologus, *Sermon 67*, "The Lord's Prayer," and *Sermon 70*, "The Lord's Prayer." Cyril of Jerusalem, *Mystagogical Catecheses*, V,11-18, "The Lord's Prayer." Gregory of Nyssa, *The Lord's Prayer*, translated and annotated by Hilda Graef, Westminster, Md.: Newman Press, 1954. John Chrysostom, *PG* 51, 29-40; 44-48; and *PG* 57, 278-282. Theodore of Mopsuestia, *Homily* XI.

[16]Augustine, *Sermon* 59, 8.

[17]For Augustine's parallel of the Lord's Prayer with the beatitudes, see his *Commentary on the Sermon on the Mount*, II,11 (38).

[18]Theodore of Mopsuestia, *Homily* XI,19.

[19]For a ceremony inspired by the presentation of the Gospels, we would recommend that instead of reading the opening verses of each gospel, the ministers proclaim Mark 1:1-5; Matt. 3:13-17; Luke 18:28-34, and John 20:30-31. For more background see Andre Laurentin and M. Dujarier, *Catéchuménat: données de l'histoire*, pp. 329-330

[20]V. de Rosa, *Fonte patristiche della Traditio Psalmorum*, Naples, 1952. See also *DACL* XV, "Scrutins" p. 1043.

[21]Jean-Paul Sanon, "Un catéchuménat d'adultes en Haute-Volta," in *Devenir chrétien en Afrique*, Recherche sur les étapes catéchétique et liturgiques de l'initiation dans la communauté chrétienne, published by La Commission de Catéchèse et Liturgie de l'Ouest Africain francophone, 1976, pp. 151-159.

Chapter 6
The Sacred Triduum

THE final period of the catechumenal preparation prior to the reception of the sacraments of initiation is sometimes called the "baptismal retreat." It begins with the celebration of the rite of Election, and is characterized by the celebration of the Presentations, and especially by the Scrutinies. It is a time of purification and enlightenment of the catechumens, and normally coincides with the season of Lent. It reaches its culmination in the solemn celebration of the sacraments of initiation, and the Easter Vigil is considered the proper time for their celebration (*RCIA*, 8, 49, 55).

But the Easter Vigil itself is but a part of what we have become accustomed to calling "Holy Week." Thus, in order to appreciate the significance of the ceremonies of initiation during the Easter Vigil, we must extend our vision to the "holy days" which immediately precede it.

The Earliest Practices of the Church: Holy Week

BEFORE describing the manner in which the Church conferred the sacraments of initiation in the earliest centuries, it would be helpful to first say something about the way in which the Church celebrated the paschal mystery.[1]

The Triduum

What we now refer to as the Easter Triduum represents the results of a long and gradual evolution of liturgical practices.

In the very earliest days of the Church, Easter was celebrated not once a year, but rather once every week. The celebration of Easter consisted of the Sunday Eucharist, which enabled the believers to relive the death and resurrection of the Lord. It was not until towards the end of the second century that it became customary to celebrate Easter as an annual event. In the East, the celebration was held on the exact anniversary date of the Resurrection, whereas in the West, the feast always fell on a Sunday.

By the third century, Easter consisted of a single celebration of both the passion and the resurrection of Christ. There was *only one* liturgical celebration: the eucharistic liturgy of the Vigil. It was on that night, and on that night *only*, that Christians celebrated the death and rising of the Lord. While there was only one liturgical celebration, the feast of Easter was understood as extending over three days, but only because the solemnity of the feast called for two days of fasting (Friday and Saturday). There was no celebration of "Holy Thursday" or "Good Friday."

These three days were called the Triduum, not in reference to any historical events connected with "Holy Thursday" or "Good Friday," but simply because of Christ's reference to his rising "on the third day." Note as well that at this epoch, Pentecost was not a special feast either; it's name simply indicates the "fiftieth day" during the prolonged period of Easter joy.[2]

It is not until the fourth century that a desire to dramatize the events of Christ's life will lead to the dismembering of the paschal mystery into its various elements, and at the cost of clouding from view its fundamental unity. The Passion came to be separated from the Resurrection: Easter was now a celebration of resurrection, and so the feast of "Good Friday" was created to celebrate the passion. And in order to have "three days," the feast of Holy Thursday was created.

This same concern of the fourth century to celebrate individual events of the life of Christ led to the solemnization of the "fiftieth day," which was originally a celebration of both the departure of Christ and the sending of the Holy Spirit. From that one celebration were carved two separate and distinct feasts: the Ascension and Pentecost.

Holy Week

In its origins, "Holy Week" was simply an extension of the two days of fasting prior to the celebration of the Vigil. In time, however, it came to be considered as the last week of Lent.

In the third century, Christians had to fast only once a year—on the two days before the celebration of the paschal mystery. But already in Egypt and Syria, there was a custom of fasting not just on the Friday and Saturday before Easter, but for the whole week previous. This corresponds to the period of prayer and fasting, described by Justin in the second century, as the community's immediate preparation for the celebration of the sacraments of initiation.

During the fourth century, the Church instituted the season of Lent, in order to foster the preparation for Baptism of catechumens who did not undergo a serious period of formation. This was also when the penitents prepared for the solemn ceremony of reconciliation which took place on Holy Thursday.

The last week of this Lenten period thus took on a special importance of its own. It is toward the end of the fourth century that the Church will solemnize the Sunday which opened that last week of Lent by reading the Passion and dramatizing the triumphal entry of Christ into Jerusalem.

The Final Preparation of Those About to be Baptized

The celebration of the sacraments of initiation was always done in a very solemn and communal fashion. Let us briefly summarize what we know about this celebration.

Second and Third Centuries: Justin and Hippolytus furnish us with the most explicit information from the second and third centuries. Justin (c. 150) distinguishes three facets of this celebration:[3]

> *The preparation of the community:* "They are taught, during the course of a fast, to pray and implore God for the remission of all their past sins, while we pray and fast with them . . ."
>
> *The baptism, done in cold running water, in the presence of only a few members of the community:* "They are led by us to the water, and according to the rite of regeneration by which we ourselves were regenerated, they are regenerated also . . . "
>
> *The solemn eucharistic celebration with the entire community:* "After being bathed the one who believes is now joined to us, and we lead him to where are assembled those whom we call brothers, fervently praying together . . ."

Hippolytus (c. 215) is even more explicit.[4] He describes an extended period of preparation by the community which appears to have taken a whole week after the election of the candidates.[5]

> "From the day on which they were chosen, may we lay hands on them everyday, thus exorcising them. As the day of their baptism approaches, may the Bishop exorcise them individually to assure that they are pure. If one of them is not pure, he is to be dismissed, since he has not listened to the Word with faith, and because the alien is still hiding

within him. Those who are to be baptized should be urged to wash and bathe on the fifth day of the week . . . All those to be baptized should fast on Friday and Saturday. On Saturday, may the Bishop gather them all together in the same place and invite them to get down on their knees and pray. In laying hands on them, may he command every foreign spirit to depart from them, never to return. When he has finished the exorcism, may he blow on their faces and after having signed them with the cross on their foreheads, ears, and nostrils, may he have them stand up. The night will be spent in listening to the readings and instructions. May those who are to be baptized bring with them only the vessel they need for the Eucharist; for it is fitting that whoever is worthy of it should offer the oblation."[6]

During the Easter Vigil, the Baptism and Confirmation took place "at the crowing of the cock." According to Hippolytus, the ceremony had the following structure:

— Disrobing.
— Blessing of the oil of graces and the oil of exorcism by the Bishop.
— Renunciation of Satan (while turning toward the West) followed by an anointing with the oil of exorcism.
— Triple immersion accompanied by a triple interrogation of faith.
— The clothing of the newly baptized and their entry into the Church.
— Confirmation by the Bishop: imposition of

hands, anointing, signation, kiss of peace.

— The newly confirmed are then permitted to join in prayer with all the faithful to whom they can now extend a kiss of peace.

Note that in the second and third centuries there was a number of variations in the above mentioned structure of the baptismal celebration.[7]

The Eucharist immediately followed the Baptism and Confirmation. After receiving the Body of Christ, the neophytes drank three cups: a cup of water, "as a sign of purification;" a cup of milk and honey, "to signify the fulfillment of the promise made to our fathers," which is realized in "the flesh of Christ given by himself, by which the believers are nourished as little children;" and finally, a cup of wine.

Thus *began* the life of the Christian, for the sacraments of initiation mark not the end of journey, but the beginning, as Hippolytus clearly emphasized: "When that is finished, may each one strive to do good works, plead to God, live well, by remaining rooted to the Church and by putting into practice what he has been taught, and by continuing to progress in the service of God."[8]

Fourth and Fifth Centuries: We possess so many documents which attest to the initiatory practice of the Church in the fourth and fifth centuries that to list them all here would simply take too much time and space. Let us rather summarize the main aspects of the paschal initiatory rites during these centuries.[9]

Recitation of the Creed: The ceremony of the recitation of the Creed was inserted, at least in Jerusalem, into the liturgy of Palm Sunday. In Rome, Milan, and certainly in Africa, it was not the recitation but the

Presentation of the Creed which took place that day.

In Spain, Palm Sunday was the occasion for the celebration of the rite of ephpheta before Mass, as a preparatory rite. But in Milan this rite took place during the Easter night, immediately before the renunciation of Satan. Elsewhere than at Jerusalem, the recitation of the Creed took place on Holy Thursday, or even on Holy Saturday, as was the case in Rome. All the other baptismal ceremonies which we will now describe took place during the Easter Vigil.

The Renunciation of Satan: The renunciation of Satan was traditional to all the Churches, although there were variations in the details of the ceremony from place to place.

In the vestibule of the baptistry, the candidate faced the West, the direction symbolic of darkness and the kingdom of Satan. He took off his outer garment and stood in his bare feet on a piece of animal hide as a sign of repentance and to show that he tramples under foot the animal skins that Adam had to wear after his fall. Then standing with arms outstretched (or on his knees with arms outstretched in prayer), he renounces Satan and all idolatrous practices and superstitions.

Allegiance to Christ: Allegiance to Christ is closely allied with the renunciations of Satan. It says in positive terms what the renunciation says in negative terms. The pact broken with Satan is replaced by one concluded with Christ. In the allegiance, the candidate turns his face to the East, the direction symbolic of Christ, the light of the world who will one day return for us. East also symbolizes Paradise which is opened to the candidate by baptism.

According to John Chrysostom, the formula for the act of allegiance was Christological: "I enter your service, O Christ." More often, however, the formula was a profession of faith in the Trinity—the same act of faith required for Baptism. Immediately after this act of allegiance, the candidates were then allowed to enter the baptistry.

The Anointing: Stripping himself of all his clothes was a sign that the candidate was stripping himself of the old man and all his practices. It also likened him to Christ, who hung naked on the cross. It was a sign that he was shedding the mortality incurred by the sin of Adam and returning to the state of original innocence.

In all the Churches, the anointing was done with the oil of exorcism, either on the forehead or on the entire body. It symbolized the healing from sin, and gave the candidate the power he would need to conquer Satan, not only for the rest of his Christian life, but especially at that moment of Baptism which is a plunging into death where Satan reigns.

In some Churches, a second anointing, *before* Baptism, was done with the oil of grace. Some considered this as a second exorcism. Others considered it as a sign of the immortality conferred by Baptism. Still others, especially in Syria, saw it as connected with the gift of the Holy Spirit.

The Baptism: The act of baptism was always preceded by the consecration of the water, since "water is the instrument, although it is the Holy Spirit who acts. The water cannot heal unless the Holy Spirit descends upon it to make it holy."[10] The blessing of the water was always preceded by an exorcism.

The rite of Baptism itself was essentially plunging

into and rising from the water, accompanied by an invocation of the Trinity. The candidate died to sin, was born to divine life by the gift of the Spirit, and became an adopted son or daughter of God.

In addition to the theme of death-resurrection,[11] the Fathers developed extensively the theme of a new birth: The Church is a mother who brings her children to birth by Baptism. This explains why the baptismal pool was often compared to a mother's womb.

In the early years of the Church, and for a long time thereafter, the baptism was done by immersion.[12] (In time, it became the custom for the priest to pour water on the person's head while the candidate stood in water up to his knees.) The immersion was done three times, as a symbol of Trinitarian faith. The triple immersion also came to be associated with the three days Christ lay in the tomb.

Each immersion was accompanied by a question asked the candidate about his faith in the Father, the Son, and the Holy Spirit. These questions were later replaced by a formula in the affirmative. But even this affirmation was spoken in the passive voice (N . . . . .is baptized in the name of the Father, the Son, and the Holy Spirit) in order to express that it is God and not the priest who acts.

Complementary Rites: Three complementary rites normally followed immediately after the Baptism. The most universal was the clothing with a white garment, which replaced the garments which the newly baptized had just discarded, which was symbolic of his dying to the old man. The new garment signified that the newly baptized was now clothed with the life of Christ. The white color recalled the glory of the transfigured Christ, his resurrection, and the victory of the elect in heaven. It was a sign of divine life more than of purity. The neophytes wore this garment for the following eight days.

In certain Churches it was customary for the bishop to wash the feet of the neophytes in order to inculcate a spirit of service desired by Christ of his followers, and as a sign of protection from sinning.

We might also mention the custom of placing a crown on the heads of the neophytes to demonstrate that the former slave to sin had recovered his freedom, and that by his Baptism, the neophyte had now become a priest.

Rite of Consignation: The rite of "sphragis" or consignation must also be counted among the most ancient of all the baptismal traditions of the Church. It has also been the subject of much discussion and disagreement among scholars, especially since some authorities hold that in certain Churches, notably in Syria and Asia Minor, the anointing with chrism was done *before* and not after the Baptism. In any case, we wish only to underline the importance of this rite which lays the foundation for the doctrine and practice of Confirmation as radically allied with Baptism (even if its administration was delayed until long after Baptism) and linked to the gift of the Holy Spirit.

Other Complementary Rites: Depending on circumstances of time and place, other complementary rites were part of the baptismal ceremony. There often was a kiss of peace given to the neophytes as they exited from the baptistry, which was distinct from the kiss of peace which would be shared during the Eucharist. The rite of the lighted candle, so popular today, does not find any explicit confirmation in the catechess of the early centuries.

Celebration of the Eucharist: The culmination of the baptismal ceremony came with the celebration of the Eucharist. As they left the baptistry, the neophytes were led in solemn procession to the place where the Eucharist would be celebrated. After their "first communion" during this Eucharist, the neophytes drank a mixture of milk and honey, which symbolized their entrance into the new promised land, their new birth, and the sweetness of Christ.

The Meaning of the Stage

IT is not our intention to present here a theology of Baptism. Rather, let us recall the fundamental significance of these rites as it is presented in the preliminary remarks of the *RCIA* (27-36, 210-212).

The third stage in the catechumecial journey is the celebration of the three sacraments of initiation. The elect pass through this stage so that "with their sins forgiven," they "are admitted into the people of God, receive the adoption of the sons of God, and are led by the Holy Spirit into the promised fullness of time and, in the Eucharistic sacrifice and meal, to the banquet of the Kingdom of God " (*RCIA*, 27).

Baptism

The Blessing of the Water: The blessing of the water is so important for understanding the sacrament of baptism that it should be done even if the baptism takes place at a time other than the feast of Easter (*RCIA*, 210). Its purpose is two-fold: It recalls "the dispensation of the paschal mystery" (*RCIA*, 29) and "the wonderful works of God from the creation of the world and the human race to the mystery of God's love" (*RCIA*, 210).

The blessing of the water also highlights the sacramental mystery of water and its relationship to the Trinity: "By calling on the Holy Spirit and by announcing the death and rising of Christ, the newness of the washing of regeneration by the Lord is taught;

through baptism we share in his death and rising and are made the holy people of God" (*RCIA*, 210).

The Renunciation and Profession of Faith: The renunciation of Satan and the profession of faith are ultimately linked together and constitute *one* rite (*RCIA*, 211). Together, they constitute an essential element of Baptism, because they express "the active faith of those to be baptized," which is both the faith of the entire Church and the personal faith of the individual. (*RCIA*, 30). "Baptism is a sacrament of faith by which the catechumens adhere to God and at the same time are given new life by him" *(RCIA*, 211).

It is fitting, then, that before Baptism, the candidates should "renounce sin and Satan completely so that they adhere forever to the promise of the Savior and the mystery of the Trinity. By this profession, which they make in the presence of the celebrant and the community, they signify their intention, brought to maturity during the catechumenate, of entering into a new covenant with Christ" (*RCIA*, 211). Thus, the newly baptized enter willingly into a covenant with Christ by "rejecting errors and adhering to the true God" (*RCIA*, 30). "They profess their living faith in the paschal mystery of Christ" and "in the Holy Trinity" (*RCIA*, 31).

The Rite of Water: Plunging into the water signifies the newly baptized's participation in the paschal mystery of Christ. The efficacy of this rite is due to the Trinity itself, who "called on by the celebrant, brings about the numbering of the elect among the adopted children of God and unites them to his people" (*RCIA*, 31).

Note well what the new Rite says, "The washing is not merely a rite of purification, but a sacrament of union with Christ" (*RCIA*, 32). The rite should then express as clearly and forcefully as possible that it is a "sign of mystical sharing in the death and rising of Christ, by which believers in his name die to sin and rise to eternal life" (*RCIA*, 33).

We do find it somewhat surprising that after stressing so much that Baptism is primarily participation in the death and rising of Christ, the new Rite continues to speak of baptism as a "washing" (*RCIA*, 28 and 31).

Three Complementary Rites: The new Rite terms the three complementary rites of anointing with chrism, clothing with a white garment, and the presentation of the lighted candle as "explanatory" rites (*RCIA*, 223), since they explain the significance of what just happened in the rite of Baptism.

The anointing with holy chrism "is a sign of the royal priesthood of the baptized and their enrollment in the fellowship of people of God" (*RCIA*, 33). Let us put this more precisely by saying that through Baptism, the neophytes become members of Christ the Priest, Prophet, and King, and thus members of the Church, they become participants themselves in this triple function of Christ (see the prayer of anointing in *RCIA*, 224).

The white garment "is a symbol of their new dignity" (*RCIA*, 33). They are clothed in Christ and have become new creatures and must live this new life until his return (*RCIA* 225).

The lighted candle "shows their vocation of living as befits the children of the light" (*RCIA* 33) so that they may one day enter with Christ into his heavenly kingdom (*RCIA* 226).

Confirmation

The sacrament of Confirmation should be administered to adults immediately after their Baptism, "according to the ancient practice maintained in the Roman liturgy" (RCIA 34). This proximity of Confirmation with Baptism serves well to manifest "the unity of the paschal mystery, the close relationship between the ministry of the Son and the pouring out of the Holy Spirit, and the joint celebration of the sacraments by which the Son and the Spirit come with the Father upon those who are baptized" (RCIA 34).[13]

The Eucharist

According to Vatican II, the Eucharist "shows itself to be the source and the apex of the whole work of preaching the gospel. Those under instruction are introduced by stages to a sharing in the Eucharist."[14]

The Eucharist is truly "the culminating point of their initiation" (RCIA, 36), the "climax of their initiation" (RCIA, 234), which is why the catechumens should participate in the Eucharist immediately after their Baptism and Confirmation, which are normally celebrated within the context of the Eucharist.

In the celebration of the Eucharist following their reception of Baptism and Confirmation, the neophytes, for the first time, have the full right to take part. Having received the dignity of the royal priesthood of Christ, they should take an active part in the general intercessions, in bringing the offerings to the altar, in participating with the rest of the community in the action of the sacrifice, in proclaiming the Lord's Prayer (made possible by their becoming adopted children of God by Baptism), and in receiving the body and blood of Christ (RCIA 36).

The Structure of These Rites

THE new Rite says nothing specific about the participation of those about to be baptized in the Holy Week ceremonies prior to the Easter Vigil. It is obvious, however, that they should celebrate them with the rest of the community since this can be of help to them in preparing for their new birth in the Church.

Before examining the structure of the Easter Vigil, let us first see what the new Rite has to say regarding the "preparatory rites" (RCIA 193-207).

Under the heading of "Preparatory Rites," the RCIA groups together a number of optional rites that can be celebrated, either in whole or in part, depending on circumstances, where it is possible to gather the elect together on Holy Saturday morning (RCIA, 193). "On Holy Saturday, when the elect refrain from work and spend their time in recollection, the various immediately preparatory rites may be performed: the recitation of the Creed, the ephpheta or the opening of the ears and mouth, the choosing of a Christian name, and even the anointing with the oil of catechumens" (RCIA 54).

The Recitation of the Creed (RCIA, 194-199): The recitation of the Creed can be celebrated at this time, on the condition that it has already been presented to the elect previously (RCIA, 195). "By this rite the elect are prepared to profess their baptismal faith and are taught their duty of proclaiming the Gospel message" (RCIA, 194).

The ceremony consists of four parts:

a. *The Readings and the Homily*
   After an appropriate song, one of the following passages is read: Mark 16:13-17; John 6:35, 63-71, or if the rite of ephpheta is to be celebrated, Mark 7:31-37.
b. *The Rite of Ephpheta* (see below)
c. *The Prayer for the recitation of the Creed (RCIA 198)*
d. *The recitation itself*

Naturally the text of the Creed to be recited (Apostles' or Nicene) should be the same as that presented to the elect earlier.

The Rite of Ephpheta (RCIA, 200-202): The rite of ephpheta signifies that the candidate's ears are open to hearing the Christian message, while his lips are ready to proclaim his faith and the glory of God. "By its symbolism, this rite shows the need of grace for anyone to be able to hear the Word of God and to work for salvation" *(RCIA,* 200). This explains why it may be well to celebrate this rite at the same ceremony in which the Creed is recited.

If the Creed is not to be recited, the RCIA proposes the following schema:

a. *Reading and Homily*
   After an appropriate entrance song, the reader proclaims Mark 7:31-37 and the celebrant explains its significance in light of the rite.
b. *The Rite Itself*
   The celebrant touches the ears of each of the elect with his thumb, and then their lips, while pronouncing the prescribed formula *(RCIA,* 202) in its entirety for the first candidate, and simply "Ephpheta, that is, be opened" for the following candidates if they are numerous.

The Choosing of a Christian Name (RCIA 203-205): We have already noted that the choosing of a Christian name can take place at the time of entrance into the catechumenate. "Where non-Christian religions flourish, which immediately give a new name to those who become members, the episcopal conference may decide that new catechumens may keep the name they already have, or take a Christian name or one familiar in their culture . . . as long as it has a Christian meaning" *(RCIA,* 88). If the choosing of a Christian name did not take place at the candidate's entrance into the catechumenate, the rite can be celebrated on Holy Saturday as follows:

a. *Reading and Homily*
   The rite begins with an appropriate song. The new Rite offers the following choice of readings: Genesis 17:1-7; Isaiah 62:1-5; Rev. 3:11,13; Matt. 16:13-18; John 1:40-42.
b. *The Rite Itself*
   The celebrant asks each candidate the name he has chosen (or the name given him by his parents earlier) and he explains its Christian meaning.

Anointing with the Oil of Catechumens (RCIA 206-207): The meaning of this anointing is recalled in ancient Christian prayers which have come down to us. The oil is reserved to those who are ready to proceed to Baptism, and is used to attest to the purity of the one about to be baptized, and to break any remaining bonds which attach the catechumen to Satan. In freeing him from Satan, the oil strengthens the candidate for the battle he must fight with Satan and with sin in the baptismal bath.

The RCIA specifies that this anointing "should signify the need of God's strength so that the person who is being baptized, despite the bonds of his past life and overcoming the adversity of the devil, may strongly take the step of professing his faith and hold to it without faltering throughout his entire life" (*RCIA*, 212).

The Place of the Rite: Normally, this anointing should be celebrated during the Easter Vigil, between the renunciation of Satan and the profession of faith. But for pastoral and liturgical reasons, the rite may be anticipated on Holy Saturday, providing that the episcopal conference has decided not to omit this rite (*RCIA*, 206 and 218).

If it is celebrated on Holy Saturday, it can be celebrated "separately, or with the recitation of the profession of faith or Creed, or it may be done before it, to prepare for the profession of faith or Creed, or after it, to confirm it" (*RCIA*, 206).

The Rite Itself: The oil of the catechumens used for this rite is blessed by the bishop at the Chrism Mass. But for pastoral reasons the priest may bless the oil during the ceremony, using the prayer indicated in *RCIA*, 207. The catechumens are then anointed individually on the breast or on both hands or even on other parts of the body if this would be appropriate. If there is a large member of candidates, several ministers may assist with the anointing.

The Easter Vigil

We will not concern ourselves here with all the ceremonies indicated for this celebration in the missal, but only with the specific aspects of the Vigil indicated by the new Rite.

The Litany: The celebration of Baptism, for which the assembly has been prepared by means of the readings, begins with the litany of the saints (*RCIA*, 213-214). This emphasizes the communal nature of the Church throughout space and time. It would be fitting to insert into the litany the names of the patron saints of those about to be baptized.

Blessing of the Water: The formula for the blessing of the water is taken from the liturgy of the Vigil service. Outside of Easter time, the water should always be blessed, using one of the formulas listed in *RCIA*, 215 and 218. During Easter time, even if the water to be used was blessed during the Vigil, it should be blessed again with a prayer modeled on the examples in *RCIA*, 389 and 216.

Renunciation of Satan: The new Rite proposes three formulas for the rite of renunciation and urges episcopal conferences to develop one or several models which take into account the local situations and problems (*RCIA*, 217). The renunciation is followed by the anointing with the oil of catechumens if this was not done before (*RCIA* 218).

Profession of Faith: The new Rite proposes only one formula for the profession of faith (*RCIA*, 219): that of the Creed in the form of three questions. Note, however, that the Rite of Confirmation, when celebrated apart from Baptism, furnishes a variety of forms for the profession of faith.

The Rite of Water: Both immersion and infusion are mentioned as possibilities for administering the Baptism. If the Baptism is done by immersion, either the entire body or just the head is submerged three times (*RCIA*, 220). Infusion consists of pouring water three times over the head (*RCIA*, 221).

The new Rite recommends the assembly participate in this rite by songs between the readings and periods of silence, and during the rite of the actual Baptism if the candidates are numerous (*RCIA*, 222). They may join in a brief sung acclamation after the Baptism of each neophyte (*RCIA*, 220-221, and 393-411).

Anointing with Chrism: The anointing with Chrism does *not* take place if Confirmation is to be celebrated as part of the rite.

If Confirmation is to be conferred, it is done by the priest celebrant if the bishop is not present. After addressing the neophytes and the congregation, the celebrant (and celebrants) impose hands over all the confirmands together, and confirms each one according to the new Rite of Confirmation.

The White Garment and Candle: The color of the garment with which the neophytes are clothed can be determined by local customs. This rite can be omitted (*RCIA*, 225). For the rite of light, the celebrant takes (or touches) the paschal candle and invites the godmothers and godfathers to light from it the candle which they themselves will give to their godchildren. After the neophytes have been presented with their candles, the celebrant says the formula indicated in *RCIA*, 226.

The Eucharist: The new Rite gives the following indications for celebration of the Eucharist: (1) The Creed is not said. (2) The neophytes participate in the general intercessions and the offertory procession (*RCIA*, 232).

(3) The Eucharistic prayer includes the special mention of the neophytes and their godparents (*RCIA*, 233, 377, 412). (4) The neophytes (together with their godparents, parents, spouses, and catechists) receive communion under both species (*RCIA*, 234).

Baptism Outside of Easter: Where, *by exception,* Baptism is celebrated outside of Easter, it is recommended that the ritual Mass for Baptism be said.[15] Note also that there exists a ritual Mass for the celebration of the rite of election and for scrutinies.

Thus far in this chapter we have examined the evolution of the Holy Week practices in the early centuries of the Church, the meaning of this culmination point of Christian initiation, and the structure of the initiatory rites of Holy Week as proposed in the new Rite. We are now in a position to look clearly at the proposed Rite from a pastoral perspective. We will attempt this in two stages: first some critical remarks on the structure, order, and time of celebration of these rites, and secondly, we will present, as examples, some concrete experiences with their implementation in order to see how these terminal rites of initiation can be enhanced by their association with the ensemble of the celebrations of Holy Week.

Some Critical Reflections on the Rites

THE *Preparatory Rites:* It seems rather difficult to celebrate all the rites of immediate preparation for Baptism on Holy Saturday as the RCIA suggests. Not only is Holy Saturday busy enough with preparations for the Vigil and Easter Sunday Masses, but it seems the very nature of the preparatory rites calls for their celebration at other times during the initiation process.

The Recitation of the Creed: The recitation of the Creed would be greatly enhanced by the presence of the entire Christian community—something which would be impossible if the rites were to be conducted during the morning or afternoon of Holy Saturday. To alleviate this difficulty, in some places the *recitation* of the Creed is deferred until the Vigil. But in so doing, the *recitation* of the Creed is being confused with *profession* of faith. The two are not the same. It would be much better to *anticipate* the recitation of the Creed on Palm Sunday, a feast which itself highlights the Creed for adhesion or allegiance to Christ in his pascal mystery. Holy Thursday might also be a fitting choice.

The Rite of Ephpheta: The rite of ephpheta has a double significance. First, the signation of the lips is connected with the candidates' ability to *profess* the faith, as indicated by the formula prescribed by the new Rite (*RCIA,* 202). It would be appropriate then to

186

celebrate this rite *before* the recitation of the Creed. Another fitting place would be during the rite of election which opens the period of the baptismal retreat. The advantage of celebrating it at that point is that it would furnish the rite of election with the visible gesture which at present is lacking in this Rite, as we pointed out in Chapter 3. Secondly, the signation of the ears expresses the "need of grace for anyone to be able to hear the word of God" (*RCIA*, 200). For this reason, it would be also appropriate to situate the rite of ephpheta at the entrance into the catechumenate to mark the candidate's readiness and ability to hear the word of catechesis.

Choosing a Christian Name: The candidate's choosing of a new Christian name (or his affirmation of the name he already has) would also profit by being celebrated at a time other than Holy Saturday. It could be done at the rite of election, since on that day God calls each of the elect by name to a deeper sharing in His divine life. Another possibility would be to express the choice of a new name during the Easter Vigil, when the candidates are reborn in Baptism. The significance of the new name could be commented upon just before the litany of the Saints—which could also include the names of the patron saints of the candidates.

Anointing with the Oil of Catechumens: The RCIA itself suggests that it would be more proper to conduct the anointing with the oil of catechumens between the renunciation of Satan and the profession of faith. Another possibility would be to anticipate its celebration during the period of the catechumenate, thus making it one of the transitional rites (*RCIA*, 127).

But even in this case, it is important to reserve a solemn final anointing toward the end of Lent to prepare the candidate for that final struggle with the devil in the baptismal rite itself. In some areas, this solemn anointing is celebrated along with the third scrutiny.

In any case, except if the rite is conducted within the Vigil, the celebrant should first bless the oil (RCIA, 207). The container should be large enough so that it is clearly visible to the assembly, and so that there will be enough oil to permit more than just a token dab of it on the forehead.

The Rites of the Easter Vigil

More than anywhere else in the new Rite, the rites of the Easter Vigil need to be reworked, both in terms of their language of expression as well as for the gestures and actions that accompany them.

Language: The prayer for the blessing of the water, while keeping its biblical flavor, should reflect more the nature of the local culture and should include acclamations by the people. The renunciation of Satan should express more clearly the very concrete practices and attitudes that the Christian must reject. The RCIA mentions superstitions, deviations, and magical acts (RCIA, 217). These examples may seem to be alien to a highly technological society. But each culture has its own devils; and they must be expressed somehow in the renunciation if this rite is to be meaningful and beneficial.

Similar adaptation must be attempted with regard to the language of the profession of faith. While the profession of faith during the Vigil is in question/

answer form, the text is virtually identical to the one the candidate already recited publicly some time earlier. Would it not be better to allow for a more personal, more developed, and more expressive solemn profession of faith than just the three "I do's" as indicated in the new Rite?

Gestures and Actions: Liturgical gestures are of particular importance in the essential action of the entire initiation process: Baptism. What then, are gestures which could best express the meaning of, for example, renunciation of Satan and allegiance to Christ?

Most importantly, however, the rite of water must clearly demonstrate the significance of death and resurrection. In cultures and areas where the celebration is conducted outdoors, a trench is dug, into which the candidates descend to be baptized.

But most churches will probably prefer to conduct the celebration of Baptism indoors. In this case, a portable baptismal pool is often placed at the head of the center aisle just below the sanctuary. The pool is usually two or three steps deep. The elect descend into the water up to their knees. Standing on one side of the pool, the celebrant pours water over the candidate's head. The godparent stands on the other side and helps them in arising from the pool. The newly baptized then enters into the sanctuary for the anointing.

The clothing with the new garment can also be an important symbolic gesture. Unfortunately, when the number of candidates is large, they are often clothed in the new garments before the ceremony begins, usually as a result of a concern for convenience or to save time. And the only clothes that are removed just before the rite of water are the candidates, shoes. In some areas of the world, the candidates are asked to come to the ceremony already wearing their new white garments but covered by an outer garment of a different color. This outer garment is removed just before the Baptism. If the aspect of nudity would make the shedding of old garments during the ceremony inappropriate, it would be better to have the newly baptized put a new white garment on *over* the old garments, rather than removing the old garment he was wearing before the Baptism.

As for the baptismal candle, the candidate should not carry their unlit candles into the ceremony. Rather the lighted candle should be given to them only after the anointing; and the candle should be lit from the paschal candle.

Marriage Within the Catechumenate

Since the catechumen is considered to be a "Christian" and already a member of the church, it is possible for catechumens to be married in the Church before Baptism. This is true for the marriage of a catechumen with a baptized Catholic, as well as between two catechumens.

Nor is there any real problem in the case of two catechumens who are already married, but whose marriage, of course, was not celebrated within the Church. If their marriage fulfills the Church's requirements for Christian marriage, then the Church considers their marriage a valid one. For this reason there is no canonical necessity to renew their marriage promises within the Church, either before or after Baptism. But from a psychological point of view, the couple may want to signify the radical change in their lives by some kind of a ceremony confirming their marriage.

In the case of a catechumen already "married" to a baptized Christian, but never married in any religious ceremony, the Church does not recognize their union as a valid marriage and requires that the couple celebrate the sacrament of marriage either during the period of the catechumenate, or at the latest, during the Vigil Service. In this case, the rite would follow the anointing immediately after the Baptism.

Celebrating the marriage during the Vigil will, of course, add yet another rite to an already ritually "heavy" liturgy, as well as lengthening it. But it does have the advantage of emphasizing that marriage is a further consecration to each other by two people who are already consecrated to the Lord and to the Christian community through baptism.

Another case which occurs more and more regularly is that of two people, *both of whom are unbaptized* and *one of whom is a catechumen,* who immediately after their engagement begin living together. We presume that the couple has the intention of marriage, although they have not yet solemnized it by any kind of religious ceremony. In this case, the marriage must be solemnized during the period of the catechumenate or at the Easter Vigil. In this ceremony, we are not talking about two people who are not yet married (as we did in the previous example) but who have entered into a common law marriage, or a civil marriage. Thus, the ceremony during the Vigil is not that of the celebration of the sacrament of marriage, but of the renewal of the promise of fidelity, and adding to that promise (if the non-Christian spouse is agreeable), an explicitly stated willingness to adhere to the values of Christian marriage.

Naturally, the question of the place of marriage

within the initiation process needs a full examination of its own—which is well beyond the scope of this study. In addition to the examples of frequently encountered situations within the catechumenate, we should also note the much more diffiuclt situation involving previous marriages of those who desire to be baptized, or who have already been baptized Christian but wish to enter into full communion with the Catholic Church. Since these kinds of situations are very delicate and may take a long time to resolve, we suggest that the pastor become aware of any such possible situations as early as possible in the candidate's journey of initiation so that delay and disappointment may be avoided as much as possible.

Pastoral Experiences of Christian Initiation within the Context of Holy Week

THE active participation of catechumens in Holy Week service provides us with a number of examples of how the rites of Christian initiation can play the central role they should within the context of all the Holy Week services, but especially within the celebration of the Vigil. In this closing section let us look at some of these examples.

The Beginning of Holy Week: In some places, particularly in Africa, Lent is a time of "baptismal retreat" in a very strict sense. During this time, the candidates have been separated from the community, similar to the period of separation and meditation that marks so many tribal initiation practices. Thus as Holy Week approaches and Lent draws to a close it is necessary to celebrate in a solemn way the end of this period of separation by the re-entrance of the elect into the midst of the community with whom they will celebrate the major rites of initiation at the end of Holy Week.

The ceremony used in these areas focuses on two essential aspects: the communal dimension of initiations, and the definitive commitment to be made by those now ready for Baptism.

To express the communal dimensions, all the community gathers with those in charge of the catechumenate around the priest or bishop who presides. The catechumens then enter the church in procession, a sign of their return from their place of retreat, carrying the large crucifix which was present with them during their period of separation. The catechumens are then welcomed back and received by the community.

The ceremony then centers on the definitive commitment the elect will soon make through their Baptism. The meaning of this commitment is explained by means of a dialogue between the celebrant and the person who was responsible for the elect during their period of retreat. The commitment is expressed by the candidates in the recitation of previously selected texts appropriate for Christian initiation and commitment (John 1, the Beatitudes, or 1 Cor. 13). Then the elders of the community as well as the celebrant clarify the meaning of these texts and urge the candidates to live them.

The action chosen to accompany this rite and to concretize all that has just been said is the blessing of the initiation crosses which each candidate takes with him and displays at home.

Such a celebration could easily be adapted to local circumstances and culture. As for the time of celebration, there are several possibilities. It could be done on Monday, Tuesday, or Wednesday of Holy Week, although this would de-emphasize somewhat the celebration of Palm Sunday by placing it before (and thus outside) the Holy Week ceremonies of initiation. Thus a more fitting time for this "re-entrance" rite would be on the evening before Palm or Passion Sunday. Still better—and easier—would be at the beginning of the Palm Sunday liturgy. The procession of the candidates from their place of quiet retreat, the carrying of the cross, and re-entrance into the church—the place of initiation—would be easy to understand in the light of the celebration of Palm Sunday.

Holy Thursday: It is important to use the initiation rites of Holy Week, not as a series of separate ceremonies, but as one ceremony which begins on the evening of Holy Thursday and which extends over the next three days. Again by way of example, we will refer to the practice of the communities of Ouagadougou, along with the personal reflections of this author.

The initiatory tone and meaning of this three-day celebration must be set by the homily at the Holy Thursday liturgy. It is on this night that the Chruch celebrates both *the Exodus,* when through a ritual meal God brought salvation to the people of Israel, and *The Eucharist,* the paschal meal in which Christ gives us the gift of his body and blood—the saving food and the sacrament of love and union which unites the Church, the people of God (1 Cor.).

This night the Church also recalls the example of service given by Christ to His Church by washing the feet of his disciples. This is the night when Judas, turning his ears not to Christ but to Satan, refused the salvation, love, union and the example of humble service offered by Christ. Instead Judas betrayed Him, and alienated himself from the ecclesial community.

Consequently, for Christians today, and especially for the catechumens, this is the night when we declare ourselves either for salvation, love, union and service to others, *or,* for death, hatred, alienation, and selfish individualism. Each one must choose Christ and His Church, the people of God, the bond of union and love, or else declares himself against Him.

Because of this initiatory significance of Holy Thursday, it would be appropriate to situate within this liturgy some of the preparatory rites of Baptism, if they have not already been celebrated before, such as:

— the rite of ephpheta;

— the recitation of the Creed and the Lord's Prayer;

— the personal journey of each candidate towards Baptism, which can be expressed by the candidates writing their names on a small piece of paper and then dropping them into the baptismal font;

— the renunciation of Satan (turning toward the West) and allegiance to Christ (turning toward the East);

— anointing.

After the Liturgy of the Word and the celebration of the preparatory rites, the catechumens would be dismissed, since they can not yet *participate* in the Liturgy of the Eucharist.

We should point out that the rite of the washing of the feet poses a number of questions regarding both its form and its meaning for the catechumens.

The meaning of the rite is clear: Christ's invitation to us to serve one another. But Christ himself tied this example of service to the Eucharist. Thus even though the catechumens usually should not be present for the Liturgy of the Eucharist, nevertheless, the rite expresses beautifully the very style of life to which they will soon commit themselves in Baptism, and in which they will then participate.

As for the form of the Rite, its significance is diminished in cultures where it is not customary for guests to have their feet washed by a servant. For that reason, some might prefer a rite of washing the hands, in cultures where this is done not by the host but by one of the servants.

Good Friday: In the rites practiced by communities of Ouagadougou, the celebration of Good Friday has been adapted to better express our *union* with Christ in his death and burial. The catechumens participate in the service, but do not play any particular role.

It has been suggested, however, that special attention be accorded them during the course of the ceremony by reserving for this service either (1) the rites of renunciation of Satan and allegiance to Christ, and the rite of anointing (instead of celebrating them along with the other preparatory rites on Holy Thursday); or (2) the blessing of the crosses which the candidates then take home and display—instead of celebrating this earlier in Holy Week as suggested above.

The Easter Vigil: We will not consider all the details of this ceremony, but limit ourselves to a few simple suggestions.

First of all, the service of light which is tied to the proclamation of Easter tidings would be better placed after the readings from the Old and New Testaments, rather than before. Common sense suggests this, and experience confirms it.

The service of light's current position at the very beginning of the Vigil stems from an ancient custom of first blessing the lamps and candles which would supply the light for the assembly. But the significance of the service of light is otherwise. It is directly tied to the solemn proclamation of the resurrection. Its logical place would be after the Vigil Service, between the proclamations of the gospel and the chanting of the Exultet.

The Mossi people in Africa light the Easter fire in the baptistry at the end of the Gospel, and the entire community begins to sing. This is followed by a brief homily explaining the meaning of the rite. Then comes the rite of Christ the Light, which includes the blessing of the new fire, a proclamation of the victorious titles of Christ, and the blessing of the paschal candle, symbol of the resurrection, enthronement of the Paschal candle, and the proclamation of the Exultet, the joyful message of resurrection.

Secondly, the rite of Baptism should clearly express that it includes not just those to be baptized, and their spouses and godparents, but includes the entire community. True, the catechumens are the recipients of the new birth, but the faithful also are given the opportunity to renew their own baptismal promises and celebrate *their own rebirth*.

The practices of the Mossi people gives us several examples of how to invest the liturgy of Baptism with its full significance.

Before descending into the baptismal pool, the candidates remove their outer garments. These garments are then gathered together and burned, as a sign of the candidate's death to his old self.

In renewing their own baptismal promises, the faithful first recite the Our Father, are presented with candles lit from the paschal candle, and finally repeat their promises and are sprinkled with water.

The rite of Baptism closes with spontaneous acclamations and congratulations of the newly baptized by the community of the faithful. And the blessings which close the celebration of the Vigil are the signal for the community to break into song and dancing.

With the ceremony of reception of the sacraments of Baptism, Confirmation, and Eucharist, the journey of initiation has reached its culmination—but it continues nevertheless. Being welcomed liturgically into the community is no substitute for engaging in the life and work of the community and for understanding more deeply the faith which keeps it alive. This is the task which awaits the neophyte during the fourth and final period of Christian initiation: postbaptismal catechesis or *mystagogia*.

Notes

[1] On this question, see the French periodical *Maison Dieu* "La Semaine Sainte," n. 41 (1955,1); and "La liturgie du mystère pachal. Renouveau sur la Semaine Sainte," n. 68 (1961,3-4).

[2] R. Cabie, "La cinquantaine paschale, grande dimanche," in *Maison Dieu*, n. 83 (1965,3), pp. 131-139.

[3] For the complete texts, see A. Hamman, *La philosophie passe au Christ*, Paris: Editions de Cerf, 1957, *Littératures chrétiennes*, Vol. 63. Justin *I Apol.*, 61,65-66.

[4] *AT*, 20-23.

[5] Michel Dujarier, *Le parrainage des adultes*, pp. 231-232.

[6] *AT*, 20. Several years earlier in northern Africa, Tertullian writes along the same lines: "Whoever is going to receive baptism should pray with frequent orations, with fasts, kneeling and vigils. They will add to this the confession of all their past sins . . ." *De Bapt.* 20,1

[7] G. Kretschmar, "Nouvelles recherches sur l'initiation chrétienne,' in *Maison Dieu*, n. 132 (1977,4), pp. 7-32.

[8] *AT*, 23

[9] Without going into the more specialized studies, we recommend to the reader J. Danielou's *The Bible and the Liturgy*, Notre Dame, Ind.: University of Notre Dame Press, 1959. The essential points are presented in "L'entrée dans l'histoire du salut. Baptême et Confirmation," in *Foi Vivante*, n. 36.

[10] Ambrose, *On the Sacraments*, I,1,15.

[11] For the various symbolisms of the baptismal rite, see Th. Camelot, *Spiritualité du baptême*, Paris: Editions du Cerf, 1963, Lex Orandi, #30.

[12] However, from the end of the first century, the *Didache* indicated that if there was no running water available, the person could be baptized by pouring water on the head. See *Didache*, 7,3.

[13] "In certain cases, Confirmation may be postponed until near the end of the period of postbaptismal catechesis or mystagogia, for example, Pentecost Sunday" (*RCIA* 56).

[14] "Decree on the Ministry and Life of Priests, 5, in *The Documents of Vatican II*, edited by Walter M. Abbott, S.J., London: Geoffrey Chapman, Ltd., 1967, p. 542.

[15] See the Roman Missal, English Edition, for ritual Masses for the Baptism of adults (the rite of election, the scrutinies, and Baptism) and the ritual Mass for Confirmation.

Chapter 7
The Period of
Postbaptismal Catechesis
(Mystagogy)

OUR study of the periods and stages which mark the journey of Christian initiation would be incomplete if we stopped at the rites of the paschal vigil presented in the previous chapter. While the Easter Vigil represents the culmination of the initiation journey, that journey continues into what the new Rite calls the period of "Mystagogia" or postbaptismal catechesis (*RCIA*, 37-40; 235-239).

"Mystagogia" is hardly a household word. "Postbaptismal catechesis" also causes questions: After two or three years of catechesis, prayer, and study, of reception of Baptism, Confirmation, and Eucharist, what is there left to learn? And what is a "neophyte"?

Because the meaning of this period and even the vocabulary which characterizes it are so unfamiliar to most people, we will depart from our usual format in this final chapter. Instead, we will begin by considering pertinent texts of the new Rite itself, in order to see more clearly just what "mystagogia" is all about This clarification will enable us to trace its earliest roots in the practice of the Church . Finally we will offer some suggestions which can guide our pastoral practice concerning the newly baptized .

Postbaptismal Catechesis in the RCIA

In contrast to its rather lengthy development of the first three catechumenal periods (evangelization and precatechumenate, catechumenate, and the time of purification and enlightenment), the RCIA speaks only briefly of the fourth period—mystagogia or postbaptismal catechesis. In this section we will consider two basic questions: What is the meaning or significance of this period? and What are the rites proper to it?

The Meaning of the Postbaptismal Period

The RCIA gives a descriptive definition of the period:

> "The community and the neophytes move forward together, meditating on the Gospel, sharing in the Eucharist, and performing works of charity. In this way they understand the paschal mystery more fully and bring it into their lives more and more" (3).

Note that the text indicates both the goal of this period and the means for attaining it: The goal is to enable the newly baptized to acquire a more profound experience of the paschal mystery, both on an intellectual level as well as on the level of lived personal experience. The means for attaining this goal are principally three: (1) meditation on the Gospel; (2) participation in the Eucharist; and (3) practicing charity and doing good works.

The new Rite (38,39) places the goal and means of the postbaptismal period within the context of the personal experience of the neophyte and the communal experience of the faithful. Let us look at each of these dimensions—the personal and the communal—of the postbaptismal period.

The personal dimension is perhaps the more obvious, since Christian journeying is an intimately personal and individual phenomenon. While the faith and example of the community are of crucial importance for the faith and insight of the individual catechumen, they can never replace it. This is why we showed at the very beginning of our study just how crucial the period of precatechumenal search and discovery is and how determinative it is for the entire catechumenal journey. Thus, the fruits of the catechumenal journey are also personal. It is the newly baptized who, through the reception of the sacraments, personally tastes the joy of the Word and the Holy Spirit. He will deepen this experience by continuing to meditate on the Word, always open to new insights, interpretations, and applications to his life, to receive the sacraments, and to live the Christian life. By means of this progressive and continuing growth, his faith will be strengthened and renewed.

But our study has also shown that personal faith needs the support of a faith community, just as the faith community needs the presence of the catechumens to continually renew itself and to keep it from taking its faith for granted. Thus there is no question of considering the catechumens simply as the "receivers" of faith, while the community is the "giver." Both give. And both receive.

It is in this sense that the Rite refers to the communal experience of faith in the postbaptismal period: "The time of postbaptismal catechesis is of great importance so that the neophytes, helped by their sponsors, may enter into a closer relationship with the faithful and bring them renewed vision and a new impetus" (RCIA, 39). Thus, it is not just their own faith experience which the neophytes are called to deepen during this period, but the faith experience of the community as well. And it is this communal deepening of faith which makes possible the integration of the newly baptized with the life of the community so that "the relationship of the neophyte with the rest of the faithful becomes easier and more beneficial" (RCIA, 39). And in order for the communal deepening of faith to be realized, the neophytes, from their very first steps, should "be helped carefully and familiarly in all circumstances by the community of the faithful, by their godparents and by their pastors. Great care should be taken that they obtain full and joyful insertion into the life of the community" (*RCIA*, 235).

The Rites of the Postbaptismal Period

The period of postbaptismal catechesis generally extends throughout the fifty days of the Easter season (*RCIA*, 237).

The rites which comprise this period are essentially the Sunday Masses of the Easter season. "In these celebrations, besides meeting with the community and sharing in the mysteries, the newly baptized will find the readings of the Lectionary appropriate for them, especially the readings of Year A" (*RCIA*, 40). Note that even when the postbaptismal catechesis takes place outside the Easter season, the readings for the Sunday Masses of the Easter season may (and should) be used. Since the rites of the postbaptismal period *are* the Sunday Masses, this facilitates the integration of the neophytes into the entire community, and in particular, to the worshipping community.

Those charged with the direction of the postbaptismal period should see that the neophytes participate in the Sunday liturgies along with their godparents. Special places for them should be reserved for them in the congregation. And perhaps most important of all, the homilies and general intercessions during this period should reflect both the presence and the needs of the neophytes (*RCIA*, 236).

The new Rite makes three suggestions which can enhance the significance of this period of Christian initiation:

1. *The Closing of the Postbaptismal Period*
   "To close the period of postbaptismal catechesis, at the end of the Easter season, around Pentecost, some form of celebration is held, adding external festivities according to local customs" (*RCIA*, 237).

2. *Involvement of the Bishop*
   "To develop pastoral contact with the new members of his Church, the Bishop should make sure, especially if he cannot preside at the sacraments of initiation, that at least once a year he meets the newly baptized and presides at a celebration of the Eucharist" (*RCIA*, 239).

3. *Anniversary Celebrations*
   "On the anniversary of their baptism, it is desirable that the neophytes gather together again to give thanks to God, to share their experiences with one another, and to gain new strength" (*RCIA*, 238).

Origins of the Postbaptismal Period of Catechesis

As we have seen throughout our study, the developments of catechumenal practices in the history of the Church can guide us in our efforts to understand and implement the practices suggested by the new Rite.

This is equally true for the practices characteristic of the postbaptismal period. But the particular difficulties we encounter in examining the historical roots of this period are: (1) two different types of postbaptismal catechumenates, and (2) differences in vocabulary and terminology for various aspects of the postbaptismal catechesis.

Was There Ever a "Postbaptismal Catechumenate"?

If by the term "postbaptismal catechumenate" we mean a structured institution, we are talking about something which never existed in the history of the Church. But this does not mean that the Church did not exercise particular concern for the newly baptized.

We can begin to clarify the circumstances which gave birth to postbaptismal catechesis by distinguishing between two historical periods. During the first three centuries, in which the Christian community played a very active role in the formation of the catechumens, there was simply no need for any special structure to continue that formation after their Baptism. The kind of support characteristic of the process before Baptism was equally visible after it.

But in the fourth century, this situation is no longer the case. By this time, the formerly long period of catechumenal formation had been reduced to the few weeks of Lent. The Church prolonged this insufficient period by adding an extra week after the Baptism of the catechumens, calling this extension the "week *in albis*". This refers to the white garments worn by the neophytes for the week following their Baptism.

Up to this point we have been referring to the newly baptized as the "neophytes." But other names for the newly baptized were used—in different times and places—each of which reflected a different perspective on Baptism.

Seeing Baptism primarily as a sacrament which gives *new life* led to the rise of the two most popular terms to designate those who had just been baptized. "Neophyte" (*neophutos*), following the line of thought in Tim 3:6, emphasized that the newly baptized had been given a new nature, since Baptism makes of us new creatures.[1] The "newly enlightened" (*neophotistos*) was the other most popular term. Reflecting Ephesians 5:8, this term emphasized the fact that the individual has received the light of truth, has become enlightened and illuminated.[2]

Baptism was also seen by the early Church as a rebirth. This aspect of Baptism, in line with 1 Peter 2:2, gives rise to the term "infant"—from the Latin *infans*, meaning one who cannot yet speak. Augustine tells us that this term was not reserved for babies, but was used to designate the newly baptized who were adolescents, young adults, and the elderly alike.

We have mentioned that the newly baptized donned a white garment (*alba; vestis candida*) for the week following. This practice gave rise to yet another name for the newly baptized: "albati" or "candidati."

The Postbaptismal Catechumenate in the First Three Centuries

Until Constantine ended the long period of persecution, there was no such institution or structure known as the postbaptismal catechumenate. Up to this point, the neophytes were allowed into the community, which continued to exercise special care and support for them as a matter of course. The Liturgy of the Word and the homilies continued to be directed to them.

Integration into the Community: The complete integration of the neophytes into the community was most visibly expressed by the full participation of the neophytes in the entire Eucharistic Liturgy. The Acts of the Apostles cite example after example of communal life after Baptism. Acts 2:42, which describes that communal life, should be understood within the immediate context of Acts 2:37-41. Acts also relates how the neophytes spent several days with the brothers (Acts 9:19; 10:48; 16:15) and how they shared with the faithful in the Eucharist (Acts 16:34).

Justin also witnesses to the integration of the neophytes into the community. In his time—the second century—it was customary to celebrate Baptism at a place of running water—which usually meant at a place different from the Church or where the community regularly gathered for the Eucharist. This distance made necessary a procession from the place of Baptism to the place of Eucharist. It is in describing this procession that Justin gives us an example of how the early Church took her new members immediately to her heart:

> "After having washed the one who believes and having joined him to ourselves, we lead

him to where those whom we call our brothers are assembled. We pray together fervently, . . . then we give each other the kiss of peace. (The Eucharist then follows)".[3]

Another source for our knowledge of how the early Church integrates her new members into the community through the Eucharist is the Apocrypha, specifically the apocryphal Acts of the Apostles and the Clementine writings.[4] Likewise, Tertullian said to those about to be baptized: "You are going to rise from the holy bath of new birth. For the first time you will then join your hands with a Mother (i.e., the Church) and with brothers (i.e., the Community)".[5]

The Care and Support Extended by the Community: The community's concern for neophytes was clearly manifested by the homilies and the communal catechesis. Two fine examples of postbaptismal catechumenal homilies have come down to us from the second century. By "catechumenal homilies" we should not understand that the general community of the faithful were not present, but that in the midst of the worshipping community special attention was drawn to the needs of the newly baptized. The so-called Second Epistle of Clement is really a homily, given most likely in Corinth around the year 150—the most ancient Christian homily we possess. It stresses (1) the image of the Church as mother, who has given birth to us; (2) the seal of Baptism which we must strive to keep intact; (3) the necessity of charity. In all likelihood, it was directed particularly to the neophytes.[6]

A little known fragment from the writings of Clement of Alexandria[7] gives a beautiful example of an exhortation to live the Christian life. It is subtitled

"Counsels for those who have just been baptized."
Among these counsels we find a passage dealing with
the newly baptized's need to live entirely for Christ:

> "May all actions and all words be turned
> toward God. Bring all your concerns to
> Christ, and at every instant, turn your soul
> toward God. Base all your reflection solidly
> on the power of Christ, so that it may rest
> calmly, sheltered from the waves of all need-
> less talk and agitation, in the divine light of
> the Savior. Day after day, share your thinking
> with men, but join it to that of God, during
> the day as well as at night. Do not let yourself
> fall into a deep sleep which closes your eyes
> and deadens your mind to prayers and
> hymns, for this kind of sleep is a prelude to
> death. Keep yourself always in active union
> with Christ who sends you from heaven his
> brilliant light. May Christ be your constant
> and unending joy."

As we have already indicated, catechesis was very
much part of the formation of the neophytes, for
Baptism is a birth which calls for growth, a life which
must continually mature.

It is this theme of continual growth which St.
Cyprian stresses in all of his catechesis as bishop of
Carthage. He develops a spirituality of becoming,
based on Baptism on one hand, and eschatology on
the other. He calls Christians to preserve what they
have already become by Baptism, and to appear more
and more as what they will be one day. Become what
you are; and be already what you will become.

> "We who have been sanctified by baptism
> pray that we may persevere in what we have

begun to be . . . By the mercy of God, we have been regenerated, we have been reborn in spirit. Let us imitate, therefore, what we will be."[8]

From the Fourth to the Sixth Centuries: The custom of celebrating the octave of Easter as the week "in albis" or as the "octavae (dies) infantium," during which neophytes gathered daily to receive "mystagogical" catechesis,[9] began during the fourth century. Let us examine briefly the rites and catechesis of this period.

The Rites

Clothing with the White Garment: The practice of clothing the neophytes with a white garment following their Baptism is not clearly attested to until the fourth century. Before that date, historical sources can confirm only that after the bath and anointing, each of the neophytes was dressed.[10] But from approximately the year 350 onwards, many sources attest to the clothing of the neophytes with a white garment—both in the East as well as the West—and this custom continued to be observed for a long time afterwards.

Generally speaking, the neophyte wore the white garment both at the community assemblies as well as at home. This custom was observed even if the neophyte was baptized outside of the Easter season.

In certain areas of the Western Church, there also developed the practice of placing a white band around the neophyte's head.[11] In the East, this practice was paralleled by placing not a head band, but a crown on each neophyte.

Daily Reunions: Everyday during the Easter Octave, the neophytes and their godparents gathered for catechesis and celebrations, the content and format of which varied from one area to another.

But in spite of all the variations in practice, one common denominator was the daily celebration of the Eucharist, which was celebrated at a different church each day. Each day was marked by a solemn procession to the church selected for that day, as well as procession to the place for evening prayer. It was in the course of these celebrations that the mystagogical catechesis took place, including sometimes a pilgrimage to the baptistry.

For a concrete example of this period of postbaptismal catechesis, we have the testimony of Egeria, who describes the practice in Jerusalem at the end of the fourth century:

> "When the days of Easter come, during the eight days, that is from Easter until the octave, after the dismissal from the church, we go while singing hymns to the Anastasis, where we pray and the faithful are blessed. The Bishop stands . . . and explains all that was done at baptism. At this time, no catechumen is permitted to enter into the Anastasis. Only the neophytes and the faithful who want to hear the mysteries explained can enter. The doors are closed so that no catechumen may enter. While the Bishop explains all these things, the people shout out loud their approval so that even outside the church the cries of the faithful can be heard. He unveils all the mysteries so well that no one can remain unmoved by what they hear."[12]
> And after this explanation, the neophytes still gather together later for evening prayer.[13]

The Removal of the White Garments: In most

Churches, the neophytes removed their white robes after vespers on Saturday evening. Later on, in certain areas, this was done on Sunday. Still later, there developed the practice of blessing at this ceremony the water in which the robes would be washed.

The Significance of the White Garment: The Scriptures furnish us with a number of texts which can serve as a basis for the several interpretations of the significance of the white garments. The neophytes "have clothed themselves with Christ" (Gal. 3:27); "have been enlightened"(Eph. 5:8);" have entered into the Kingdom with their robes washed white with blood of the Lamb" (Rev. 7:13-14). The most basic interpretation of the significance of the white garment is that it is a sign of the new life received in Baptism which the neophytes must strive to keep unblemished. This is the interpretation given by Cyril of Jerusalem:

> "Now that you have divested yourself of your former clothes and have clothed yourselves in spiritual white ones, you must always be clothed in white. By no means do we want you to understand by this that your clothes must always be white; but that you must be clothed with true whiteness and with spiritual splendor, so that you may say with blessed Isaiah: 'My soul rejoices in the Lord, for he has clothed me with the garment of salvation and has wrapped me in a tunic of joy.'[14]

The Catechesis: During the week following Easter, the preaching was directed to the mystery of the Christian life, both in terms of the neophyte's sacramental life and experience as well as the new kind of behavior which he should now manifest. Throughout the week the bishop brought all the catechetical preparation of the neophytes to its culmination before they returned to their villages and homes.

The Readings: The Scripture readings for this week were essentially the testimony of those who had seen the risen Christ.[15]

Mystagogical Catechesis: The mystagogical catechesis were spiritual commentaries on the rites of initiation based on biblical themes and which were intended to encourage neophytes to persevere in their new life.

Moral Catechesis: Some of the catechetical lessons of Easter week, as those of John Chrysostom, were not mystagogical in the strict sense, but were devoted to explaining the essential rules of the spiritual life.[16] They tend to deal a lot with the power of Satan, who tempts us even more after Baptism than before, and encourage the neophytes to remain vigilant in their combat with him throughout the rest of their lives. It was not Baptism itself which brings salvation, but living a baptismal life, a theme which is vividly presented in the writings of John Chrysostom:

> "Paul is not content to say 'all those who live in the Spirit of love,' but rather 'all those who are led by the Spirit of God.' According to him, the Spirit of God must govern our life as a captain steers his ship, as a charioteer governs his horses. May one not simply content himself by the memory of his baptism; nor thereby consider himself authorized to live in a negligent way. You have indeed been baptized, but if you are not led by the Spirit of God, you will have lost the dignity which has been conferred upon you,

as well as the prestige of divine adoption."[17]

The Element of Secrecy: We have seen that an aura of secrecy surrounded the mystagogical catechesis in that no one who was not already baptized was allowed to hear it. This *disciplina arcana* was characteristic of the first few centuries of the Church. In order to avoid any misunderstanding on this point, a few words of explanation are in order.

Christianity is, first and foremost, a religion of *revelation,* not of secrecy. It calls for proclamation from the rooftops. It is also a *mystery,* but a mystery which must be known and lived. The element of secrecy was a safeguard that what was revealed was revealed only to people who had the faith to accept it and live it. It was not as important to understand it as it was to live it.

In any case, we must not confuse the *disciplina arcana* of early Christianity with the pagan and gnostic religions which saw their religion and belief as secret and which could be divulged only to the elite. This kind of religious secrecy has always been in direct opposition to Christian faith.[18]

Commemoration of Baptism: Let us close this section by directing our attention to certain customs which developed, some of them rather late—relative to the early Church—as a means of commemorating one's Baptism, after one year, or every year, or in some areas, every Sunday.[19]

Anniversary celebrations (pascha annotinum): We can trace the custom of celebrating the first (or subsequent) anniversary of Baptism back as far as the seventh century. During Easter week, when the neophytes made their pilgrimage to the baptistry, we know that some of the faithful accompanied them to celebrate the anniversary of their own Baptism as well. This practice became widespread in the Western Church, and lasted as long as the Church continued to baptize (even if those to be baptized were only infants) on Easter. The day was marked by a special Mass and office celebrated by the community. Later on, the communal element dropped out of this custom, and the special Mass was replaced by a votive Mass celebrated privately.

Renewal of Baptismal Promises: The more recent practice of renewing one's baptismal promises undoubtedly grew out of the custom described above. During the seventeenth century in France, Christians were invited to renew their baptismal promises together at retreats and parish missions. Soon this was done systematically on the occasion of the celebration of first communion for children.

Since the restoration of the Easter Vigil by Pius XII, this beautiful custom has again become universal: all Christians now celebrate each year the anniversary of their spiritual rebirth by renewing their profession of faith in the presence of the neophytes during the Easter Vigil.

Weekly Commemoration of Baptism: The faithful are also invited to commemorate their Baptism at every Sunday Eucharist. This is the significance of the aspersions with blessed water which is one of the options for beginning Mass and which stresses that the eucharistic life the community is about to celebrate has its source in Baptism. The sprinkling of the blessed water on all the people within the context of the Eucharist is a far more appropriate reminder of Baptism than individuals blessing themselves with it on entering and leaving the church.

The Postbaptismal Catechumenate Today

In today's attempts to restore the ancient process of Christian initiation, there are a variety of ways in which the postbaptismal period is developing. All we can do here is to indicate some of the main tendencies of this development.

The Postbaptismal Period: To date, three models for the postbaptismal period seem to have surfaced. The first is what we may term the "baptismal retreat model." In this model, those about to be baptized, after an intense experience of Lent, gather during Holy Week to celebrate the Triduum. This retreat is prolonged for three full days after Easter. Together they deepen their understanding of the three sacraments they have just received, and celebrate the removal of their white garments at the end of the retreat, that is, on Easter Wednesday.

A second model for the postbaptismal period is the "Easter Season" model. Unlike the baptismal retreat model where the neophytes spend three full days living, studying, and praying together, this second model relies on regular meetings of the neophytes from Easter to Pentecost. In some areas, these regular meetings constitute a truly mystagogical catechesis. In others, the time is spent in intense preparation for Confirmation, which the bishop usually celebrates during the days of Pentecost.

During this period, the Masses celebrated are of two kinds, the regularly scheduled Sunday Masses for all the faithful; and special Masses for the neophytes which can serve to introduce them to as well as explain liturgical experience. Time is also taken during this period to prepare them for their first celebration of the sacrament of reconciliation.

A third model which is developing is that of the "postbaptismal year." Particularly in areas where it is customary to defer Confirmation until one year after Baptism, the neophytes attend their reunions for ongoing formation throughout the year.

The atmosphere of these meetings should be more one of prayer and sharing of experiences of the Christian life than one of instruction. The neophytes gather in small groups and meet less frequently than they did during the catechumenate. Often, these small groups continue to meet long after the postbaptismal year is over. The participation of Christians already baptized for several years can give a sense of support and encouragement.

Celebrations of the Postbaptismal Period

In addition to the celebration of Easter Monday, which is a solemn event in many areas of the world, there are two types of celebrations which mark this period: the "celebration of the neophytes," and the renewal of baptismal promises.

The Celebration of the Neophytes: The period of mystagogical catechesis closes, either after Pentecost or after Confirmation, with the celebration of the neophytes. This celebration takes various forms from one region to another. It is marked by a joyful and communal celebration of the Eucharist with the participation of the neophytes, their godparents, and families, and by all the parishioners who can come.

Renewal of Baptismal Promises: On the Easter which follows their initiation into the Church, the neophytes gather to celebrate their first solemn renewal of their baptismal promises. Special efforts should be made during Lent to enable all the members of the parish to prepare actively for their profession of faith which will take place at the Vigil service.

Some parishes also solemnly celebrate the fifth, tenth, and twentieth anniversaries of Baptism. All the members of the faithful who will celebrate a solemn anniversary that year form small groups and participate in days of recollection and a communal retreat. This is also a good way of inaugurating and establishing postbaptismal stages which are necessary if one wants to grow continually in the Christian life. Such periodic celebrations can also coincide with celebrations which publicly recognize the ministries and vocations which the former neophytes have been called to and have accepted.

Notes

[1]Cf. Tertullian, *De praescriptione haereticorum*, 41, 17.

[2]Justin, *I Apol.*, 65; Methodius, *Symposium*, 8,6.

[3]Justin, *I Apol.*, 65.

[4]Michel Dujarier, *Le parrainage des adultes*, pp. 297-328.

[5]Tertullian, *De Baptismo*, 20, 5.

[6]V. Pavan, "Battesimo e incorruttibilitã nella II Clementis, catechesi ai neofiti," in *Vetera Christianorum*, 14 (1977), pp. 51-67.

[7]See *Clement of Alexandria*, with an English translation by G.W. Butterworth, New York: G.P. Putnam's Sons, 1919. Contains the Exhortation to the Greeks, The Rich Man's Salvation, and the fragment of an address entitled To the Newly Baptized.

[8]Cyprian, *The Lord's Prayer*, 12 and 36. On this subject, see M. Reveillaud, *Saint Cyprien: l'oraison dominicale*, Paris: Publications Universitaires de France, 1964, pp. 47-48.

[9]The best researched and documented study on this subject remains the article written in 1907 by P. Puniet: "Aubes baptismales," in *DACL*, I,1, col. 3118-3140, to be complemented, of course, by more recent articles.

[10]Note that in the West, the newly baptized were dried off before putting on the white garment. This was not done in the East, so as not to wipe off the oil with which they were just anointed.

[11]Augustine, *Sermon 326, PL* 39, 1669.

[12]*Pilgrimage of Egeria*, 47.

[13]*Ibid.*, 39.

[14]Cyril of Jerusalem, *Mystagogical Catecheses*, IV,8.

[15]A serious study was done, using the writings of Augustine by S. Poque: "L'octave des nouveaux-nés," in *Augustin d'Hippo—Sermons pour la Pâques*, in *Sources chrétiennes*, 116, pp. 85-115.

[16]A listing of the principal examples of mystagogical catecheses available in English would include the following: Cyril of Jerusalem, *Mystagogical Catechesis*, in which he gives two catecheses on Baptism, one on Confirmation, and one on the Eucharist. Ambrose of Milan, *On the Sacraments. On the Mysteries*, in which homily 3 and homily 8 were given during Easter Week. Augustine, *The Easter Sermons*. Theodore of Mopsuestia, *Catechetical Homilies*, of which #12 and #14 treat Baptism, and #15 and #16 deal with the Eucharist.

[17]John Chrysostom, *Epistle to the Romans*, Homily 14. Also see Cyprian's *Scripture Testimonies Against the Jews*, *(Test. ad Quir.)*, III,26:

"Baptism and Eucharist are not enough; good works are necessary."

[18]We recommend that the reader consult the classic article by P. Batiffol, "Arcane," in *DTC* I, 1738-1758, written in 1903. However, we must be cautious of emphasizing too much the aspect of secrecy, as this article does. This overemphasis results from an examination of catechumenal practices beginning in the fourth and following centuries—the period during which the catechumenate went into decline.

[19]See B. Fischer, "Formes de la commémoration du baptême en occident," in *Maison Dieu*, 58, pp. 111-134.

[20]Cyprian, *On the Unity of the Catholic Church*, 5.

Postscript

As we close this historical and pastoral study of the liturgical stages of the Christian initiation of adults, we will make no conclusions about the usefulness of this Rite. The text and the practices speak for themselves. Those who have tried to penetrate the spirit of the new Rite and to implement it know by their own experience its value, not just for catechumens, but also for Christian communities themselves.

The richness and the joy which flow from the RCIA are another reason for intensifying our efforts to implement it. It is also yet another reason to give thanks to the Lord, for it is thanks to Him that, in the words of Saint Cyprian, "the Church, our Mother, by her ever growing fecundity, embraces an ever increasing multitude."[20]